Changing Pattern of Political Culture

Changing Pattern of Political Culture

P.K Mishra

Foreword by

Professor A.P. Padhi

Vice-Chancellor, Berhampur University, Orissa

2000

Kaveri Books

New Delhi-110 002.

ISBN 81-7479-040-3
First Published in 2000

Published by: Rakesh Goel
Kaveri Books
4697/5-21A, Ansari Road,
New Delhi-110 002 (India).

Tel.: 328 8140, Fax: 011 719 8902
e.mail: kaveribooks@vsnl.com

Typeset by: Jitendra Kumar Singh, Delhi.

Printed at: Chawla Offset Printers, Delhi-110 052.

PRINTED IN INDIA

Foreword

India's freedom struggle, led by Mahatma Gandhi, was not just a political movement. It had also a moral and spiritual dimension, and that made it unique and great. The freedom fighters were guided by high ideals noted in India's culture and tradition. They strictly followed these ideals both in their struggle for independence and in their personal life. There was hardly any difference between their words and deeds.

For some years after independence our political leaders remained honest and dedicated, and faithful to the ideals of the freedom struggle. But before long there took place a sharp decline and deterioration in their moral standards. In general, politics drifted away from morality inflicting severe damage upon our political culture, democratic process and economy. However, a small number of leaders have been able to withstand this storm of value-decline. Though a tiny minority, they have continued to abide by the Gandhian ideals and values, and tried their best to lead the people on the path of virtue and service. While at the national level the best examples of such leaders were Vinoba Bhave and Jayaprakash Narayan, in each State there were also a few leaders of moral stature. Some of these provincial leaders might have been "invisible" to the people of other States, but, through their unassuming style and silent service, they have significantly contributed to our democratic culture which is still alive in spite of continuing erosions. One such leader is Prasanna Kumar Dash of Orissa, who was a freedom fighter and has been at the centre-stage of State politics for a long period. The book, *Changing Pattern of Political Culture: 1939 to 1999,* throws sufficient light on the politics of Orissa during the long period of six decades through focussing on the life and achievements of P.K. Dash, a political leader of rare qualities, ideals and achievements.

Fifty years of Indian republic have passed with a sense of pride and frustration when the largest democracy of the world starts feeling about the inadequacies of her Constitution which has undergone large number of amendments since its introduction. The perceptions of a nation and her people change with time and situation. While the Prime Minister, A.B. Vajpayee thinks it appropriate to review the working of the Constitution, President, K.R. Narayanan in his recent Republic Day address asked a valid point, whether the Constitution has failed to meet the expectations of the Founding Fathers or the people have failed to rise to the occasion? This controversy is now uppermost in the minds of the law-makers and political thinkers of the country.

India, at the time of her struggle for freedom from British Colonial rule and even today as a free country, appears to have resorted to different social values and political norms. Gandhiji's ideology and programme of social reconstruction do not carry much weightage in the National Congress today. The ardent followers of Gandhian principles of austerity and self-sacrifice are treated with disdain and ridicule as unfortunate anachronism. Since the political developments in Orissa from 1939 to 1999 present an exact replica of the above situation, the work "Changing Pattern of Political

Culture" by Professor P.K. Mishra brings under focus the national scenario in its provincial set up. In doing so, he has projected the career of Prasanna Kumar Dash whose activities oscillated between Jayaprakash Narayan's socialism and Indira Gandhi's Democratic Socialism. He had served the Orissa Legislative Assembly a record nine times as a distinguished member during 1952 to 1999 experiencing the values of opposition and constraints of the Treasury bench. He had also played the role of a Cabinet Minister and the Speaker for two terms. The events in the life of a true Gandhian have been assessed from the view point of his response and reaction, sufferings and sacrifice. His steadfast devotion to high ideals and moral principles represent the silver lining of hope in the contemporary society bereft of any ethics and code of conduct. By leading an honest life he has justified the expectations of Dr. Rajendra Prasad whose solemn warning to the members of the Constituent Assembly was,

> If the people who are elected are capable and men of character and integrity, they would be able to make the best even of a defective Constitution. If they are lacking in these, the Constitution cannot help the country.

Echoing the above cautionary words, Soli J. Sorabjee, the great Jurist and Constitutional wizard writes that:

> The painful fact is that today Constitutional morality has become irrelevant and any mention of it raises cynical laughter. Corruption, not morality or principles is the pervasive force in our political life and its worst manifestation is the spectacle of unabashed defection.

Professor Mishra has culled the materials for the book "Changing Pattern of Political Culture" from the proceedings of the Orissa Legislative Assembly, contemporary newspapers, biographies and autobiographies of leaders of Orissa. The work is a valuable addition to the study of recent history of an undeveloped State of the Indian Union and offers a critical approach to many aspects of political behaviour, both pleasant and unpleasant. I appreciate his efforts to combine history with political sociology to understand the current national predicament more intimately.

Prof. A.P. Padhi
Vice-Chancellor
Berhampur University

Preface

The province of Orissa was created on 1 April 1936 on grounds of linguistic homogeneity for the safety and development of Oriya language, literature and culture. It gave the Oriya-speaking people an identity of their own. Apropos the provisions of the Government of India Act 1935, an elected Government based on limited franchise and limited power took office under the British regime. There were many ups and downs before India finally achieved her independence in August 1947 and the Constituent Assembly drafted the new Constitution. After the General election of 1952 conducted on the basis of universal adult franchise, real parliamentary democracy came into being. The period 1935 to 1952 saw the hightide of Indian nationalism when Gandhian ideology spearheaded by the Indian National Congress formed the motive force behind all democratic experiments.

Prior to the transfer of power by the British to Indian hands, there were two types of Governments in India; one type represented direct administration of British and the other was through the native rulers. In Orissa along with the British administered districts were 26 native States ruled by the Rajas or princes. Among these native States Mayurbhanj was the largest in size, population and natural resources. Her Rajas being enlightened and liberal had introduced a progressive Government. Not only in Mayurbhanj, they also evinced keen interest in the moral and intellectual progress of Orissa. They played significant role in the development of Oriya language and literature, general and technical education, growth of Ravenshaw College and Utkal University. They took active part in promoting Oriya nationalism too. Under their stewardship the young generation also imbibed a deep sense of liberal outlook.

In 1949 Mayurbhanj merged with Orissa province after experiencing a brief spell of popular Government formed by the leaders of the Prajamandal movement. Besides Mayurbhanj, other native states had also been merged with Orissa and constituted separate districts. The experience of integration (social, economic and administrative) was not always quite pleasant.

The present monograph intends to project Mayurbhanj as an integral part of Orissa assimilated through legislative procedure in which Prasanna Kumar Dash, an eminent Prajamandal leader and nationalist had played the role of protagonist. Elected a record nine times to the Legislative Assembly, Speaker for two consecutive terms and a cabinet Minister as the culmination of his political career, he had the distinction to remain active in state politics for long sixty years (1939-99). This being the most formative period of independent India, Orissa too experienced numerous changes and upheavals in contemporary history. He had to interact with as many as sixteen Chief Ministers and an equal number of Governments, thousands of Legislators, old and young, various political drama portraying scenes of pride and glory, shame and squabbles. During this painful journey from freedom to decadence, Dash represented value-based politics of the Gandhian era whose steady deterioration through greed for wealth and lust for power heavily corroded public morale plunging it to its nadir. Blatant corruption and dishonesty in the form of patronage, nepotism and abuse of power tainted the names of Prime Ministers, Chief Ministers, Cabinet Ministers, Governors and bureaucrats both in the States and at the Centre. The Gandhian vision of Ramrajya had fallen into the abysmal depth of depravity. General elections, instead of being contested on ideological issues, have been fought and won, or contested and lost on issues revolving round conduct and corruption. Political corruption, of late, has become the order of the day. In a sense, it has become a source of power for the unscrupulous power hungry politicians at the cost of high ideals of democracy. That the present Election Commission is bent upon eradicating this social evil from India is an encouraging thing. Its success, however, depends upon a change of people's attitude.

Politics in India is a profitable industry. Political power is traded for economic gains. The Santhanam Committee report, also known as report of the committee on Prevention of Corruption, published by the Government of India in 1964, explains how in India power has paved the path towards wealth by a "subordination of political values and institutions to economic ones".

Political corruption as a baneful aspect of leadership was not unknown in India. It is an age old phenomenon crippling our society in one form or the other. No Government appears to be free of this evil. In independent India its pernicious influence has affected every walk of life. The political office holders tend to have no moral qualms to illegally seize any opportunity for material gains. Gunnar Myrdal in the *Asian Drama* would call this as "official misconduct" as it violates and undermines the established system of public order. The aphorism that 'power corrupts and absolute power corrupts absolutely' was found to be true in letters and spirit. Social thinkers, however, could not devise means to keep politics free of corruption. Yet, honesty survived as a noble principle and watchword in public life motivating some Legislators to assiduously pursue the unattainable goal.

The present study projecting the career of Prasanna Kumar Dash in the context of Orissa politics has great relevance because in the political scenario replete with corruption, Commissions of Inquiry and fall of Governments etc. the MLA of Mayurbhanj shines like a star, an apostle of high moral values in public life. Orissa has witnessed many unwelcome changes in politics, Parties and personalities in the post 1952 era when Dash steadfastly holds on to the cherished values of parliamentary democracy as an incorruptible politician. Mayurbhanj has gifted such a person to play the role of 'Caesar's wife' in State politics. This study does not intend to highlight corruption in Orissa politics, but throws light upon one man's crusade against inefficiency and opprobrious behaviour of the politicians tempted by greed for self gratification. Dash is a rare example of courage borne of conviction and suffering. As long as true democracy survives, he will remain a role model for the new generation of Legislators. It is with this modest hope the present monograph has been written to serve as a beacon light of high moral values in our murky public life.

—**Author**

Contents

1

The Prelude

Among the twentysix feudatory states of Orissa, Mayurbhanj was the foremost. In size, population and natural resources she was considered number one.[1] She was ruled by a benevolent monarchy with a progressive administration. From the time of Krushna Chandra Bhanj (1867-1882) several progressive measures were taken to modernise the administration.[2] Land revenue settlement was introduced giving proprietorship of land to the cultivators. Records were maintained in Oriya both in revenue and judiciary. Proceedings were kept in a Record room. Printing press was set up. Fortnightly reports were published. More Schools were established for the growth of education. Health department was organised. Exploitation by money lenders was checked. In the reign of Sreeram Chandra (1890-1912) modernisation was further[3] accelerated by the appointment of highly educated Bengalis as Dewans, Judges, Magistrates and Teachers. Educated Oriyas from Cuttack and Puri were appointed against suitable jobs. A High School was setup. The Baripada Municipality came into being in 1905. Railways and Telegraph were introduced. Public hygiene and sanitation received priority treatment. Compulsory vaccination against small-pox was introduced. The State

Council with the Maharaja as the Head, functioned as the highest judicial body. Irrigation projects were undertaken. A geological survey was conducted to explore mineral wealth. An agreement with Tata Iron Company was concluded to prospect iron ore mines at Badampahar and Gorumohisani. Liberal donations were granted for the Medical and Engineering education at Cuttack. As the President of the Utkal Union Conference in 1903, the Maharaja pleaded for general, technical and female education before an elite gathering of officials and non officials. He also urged for the growth of agriculture and industries. Ideal agricultural Firms were setup in the State to educate the farmers. Sericulture and cotton cultivation were introduced as new avenues of cash crops. A department of Archaeology sponsoring exploration of historical places was another aspect of the benevolent monarchy. Publication of learned treatises written by scholars added new dimension to the administration of Mayurbhanj. The State provided special protection to the rights of the Tribals. A graded Service system with provision of pension and terminal benefits for social security was implemented for the benefit of the Government employees. The State was divided into four Sub-divisions under Sub-divisional Officers with the Maharaja functioning as Chief Executive. The State gave grain loans and other agricultural loans through co-operative credit societies. The annual budget approved by the State council regulated the income and expenditure of the State. For emergencies like floods and famines Rupees Eleven lakhs was kept apart in the budget. Rule of law prevailed in the best interest of the common man. Among philanthropic and public welfare activities mention may be made of the establishment of the Jubilee Library, Parks, play grounds, Leper Asylum which earned admiration from all quarters.[4]

The reigns of Purnachandra (1920-28) and Pratap Chandra (1928-47) witnessed further modernisation and liberalism. Public supply of drinking water, electricity, street lighting, extension of railways, agrarian reforms, improvement of agriculture, State control of the distribution system of essential commodities, house building loans, indigenous banks for providing land improvement and other loans, separation of Judiciary from the Executive, giving an opportunity to the people to share in administration, extension of local-self Government were some of the positive steps taken by Purna Chandra. Pratap Chandra further democratised the State administration. He created the Department of Industrial and Economic Survey, Cottage Industries, Agriculture, organised the State Secretariat, setup Praja Sabha and Kendra Parishad in which there was increasing involvement of the people. The establishment of Mayurbhanj Kendra Parishad in 1945 was a landmark in the history of the State which gave people the privilege of self determination.[5]

Notwithstanding the above, Mayurbhanj witnessed vigorous Prajamandal agitation with effect from 1937 which culminated on transfer of power by the Maharaja to the Prajamandal leader Sarat Chandra Das.[6] The reign of Pratap Chandra was a very trying time. It was the period of nationalist struggle for freedom under the leadership of Mahatma Gandhi. The Civil Disobedience Movement and Salt Satyagraha had involved the people of the British administered area and the Garjat States alike. Since Inchudi near Balasore was the epicentre of Salt Satyagraha in Orissa, it had made an impact on the people of Mayurbhanj on account of close proximity. Young nationalists like Gourmohan Pradhan (Manitri), Panchanan Roy Sinha (Kundapara), Manmohan Dwivedi (Patisari), Sanatam Pradhan (Betnoti) and Suryamohan Das (Bhaliadiha) took an active part in breaking Salt laws at Inchudi and had been sentenced to various terms of imprisonment outside Orissa. Except Suryamohan Das, who breathed his last at Patna Jail, other nationalists returned to Orissa after serving the prison term. Gourmohan Pradhan stayed at Pharasidinga, adjacent to Balasore town, to avoid arrest (Pharasididinga was not under the British Government) and continued to propagate Congress programme in Mayurbhanj secretly. He was again arrested near Amarda and sentenced to four months imprisonment at Patna.[7]

Although the Civil Disobedience Movement came to an end after the Gandhi-Irwin Pact in 1931, the upsurge created by Salt Satyagraha did not die out completely. The message of Gandhiji and the idealism he preached through the Indian National Congress had made a deep impact on Indian mind. Since the feudatory States were inhabited by tribals and least educated people, their political awakening was slow. The restrictions imposed by the Feudal Chiefs in prohibiting the entry of Congress leaders and nationalist newspapers also contributed to the absence of national awareness. But the Post-Civil Disobedience Movement scenario was quite different. The message of Gandhiji, the social reconstruction programme and the thrill to attain freedom from foreign rule caught the imagination of the masses as never before. Nilgiri, Dhenkanal, Ranpur and Talcher opened the flood gates of political upsurge. The Rajas of these States were symbols of British rule and personification of feudal oppression. To liberate themselves from feudal tyranny and social injustice the people took resort to organised agitation. That they were inspired by the Gandhian movement of non-violent civil disobedience was quite expected and natural. But on account of the benevolent attitude of the rulers, the impact was minimal. More emphasis was given to the programme of village reconstruction, spread of literacy and prohibition. Since the Chiefs were not tyrannical, there was no question of demanding their abdication.[8]

Earlier, during the later part of the World War I, the tribals of Mayurbhanj had revolted in protest against the policy of recruitment of labour force. At that time the State was under the Court of Wards because the Chief was a minor. The British Government had taken strong measures to suppress the revolt.[9] But the incident was alive in the memory of the people. During the Civil disobedience movement the State Government had imposed prohibition order against organising mass meetings and holding of mass procession or rally.[10] The awareness about national struggle for independence had percolated to villages in the interior areas despite all care to prevent it. All agitations and meetings were ascribed to the Congress party. During the Puja holidays in 1938, Bansidhar Behera of Dhadangi, in association with a small group of Bengalis convened a public meeting at Simla.[11] But on the previous evening they were physically assaulted by the Police of Bangiriposi. Undeterred by Police atrocity the victims along with Gourmohan Pradhan, Harihar Mohanty (a Law student), Laxmidhar Pradhan, Adwitanath Lala and Radhamadhav Patnaik held a public meeting where the Youth leaders delivered inspiring speeches[12] urging upon the people to respond to the call of the nation. They also propagated Congress message in the scattered and remote villages. Siba Prasad Mohanta of Bhanjakia and Bhaktavandu Mahanta of Raruan invited Police torture for propagating Congress programme. These two youngmen belonged to the Panchpir Subdivision. Gradually the fire of nationalism spread to Kaptipada Subdivision where udala became the focal point of agitation. The number of activists began to swell.[13] For making the Tribals conversant with Gandhiji's programme of village reconstruction, the main issues were translated into Tribal language by Manika Majhi. Purnachandra Parichha brought under severe criticism the corrupt practices of Government employees, Foresters, Policemen and the *Sardars*. With the rising tide of nationalism, elite leadership came from Saratchandra Das, an Advocate of Baripada. He was invited by Ramchandra Mahapatra to address public meetings[14].

Here, it is pertinent to discuss the factors which facilitated the spread of nationalist movement in Mayurbhanj. The call of Gandhiji and the mass uprising in the adjoining British administered districts (Balasore, Midnapore) could not go unheeded. The events reported from other Orissa Garjat States had their irresistible impact on the elites. Although as early as 1895 the feudal levies like *Begar, Bethi, Magan* and *Rasad* had been officially prohibited by the Raja, the people were subjected to the custom periodically.[15] Under the Durbar administration, land revenue was collected through local agents called *Sardars*. The *Sardars* were both oppressive and autocratic. They had amassed large landed properties by questionable means and manipulation. Very often they could declare a defaulter as *Palataka* (migrant) and auction the property. According to the proceedings of the All-India States Peoples Conference there were intermediaries like the *Sardars*, *Tehsildars* and *Lakhrajdars* in the revenue administration.. They enjoyed commissions in proportion to the amount of revenue or rent which they collected.[16] This system gave enormous power to the *Sardars* in their respective *Pargana*. They collected more from the peasants despite unfavourable weather conditions, to increase their own gain. These *Sardars* had come from outside Mayurbhanj and belonged to the *Karana* caste which was famous for shrewdness. They did not hesitate to adopt coercive measures for which the people were panicky. The use of forced labour was a very common thing for them. The exploitation of the tribal people by the Sardars was at its highest in the Panchpir Subdivision on account of its distance from Baripada, the seat of administration.[17] The peasants and rural labourers were forced to work without wages during sowing season and harvesting of paddy crop. Even, the Government employees while on tour of the interior places engaged forced labour (*bethi*) for carrying luggage. Public ponds and wells were dug and public roads were constructed through *bethi*. The Pradeep Sagar (named after the Crown Prince) of Karanjia was excavated by forced labour. Another, equally harmful custom was *Shikar bethi*, when the people of the nearby villages had to help the Raja and his friends when they were on hunting expedition as a sport. Casualties among the people were not taken care of or suitably compensated. Sometimes casualties occurred while driving wild animals in the forests either in day time or night expeditions. The *Kheda* operation to catch wild elephants was a very hazardous job which the villagers were called upon to perform. There was no exemption from the duty.[18]

Other methods adopted by the Durbar Administration to exploit the people were contributions on festival occasions like Holi and Durga Puja. In the Jashipur area of Panchpir Subdivision the *Payeka Pancha* was a levy collected from each family at the rate 1 to 4 payes (*paye* is a container to measure paddy)[19].

Mayurbhanj has a sizeable number of tribal population who live on forest wealth and products. They consider it as their birth right and do not feel the necessity of seeking prior permission of the State administration. But at times for cutting a tree for making use of either as fuel or agricultural implement they were taken to task. The state insisted on paying a stipulated sum for obtaining a license to cut tree. Likewise the State introduced Lease system to earn revenue from forest wealth/products and restricted free entry of tribals to reserved forests. Collection of honey, mohua flower, sal seeds, lac and many other items provided good opportunity to earn revenue. There was a clash of interests between the State and the Tribals leading to resentment among the innocent forest dwellers. By leasing out the business on the above items to businessmen from Bengal, although the State earned good amount of revenue, the new systems was highly unfavourable to the interest of the tribals. They were exploited by outside agencies.[20]

The land revenue administration had introduced many intermediary agencies like the *Sardars* and *Pradhans*. While collecting revenue for specifically allotted villagers, they often resorted to harsh treatment and coercion. Physical punishment like carrying stones on the head or back and standing on one leg for long hours was a common practice inflicted on defaulters. For domestic animals trespassing into reserved forests or agricultural lands the rate of fine imposed was Rupees 2/- per buffalo, Rupee one per cow or ox, and paise 50 per calf, goat, sheep etc.[21]

Though the rate of interest on loan was fixed by the State, the moneylenders often violated the rules. Some of them were charging excessive rates showing disregard to State administration and there was no preventive measure against them. In case of failure to pay the interest, the loanee invariably lost his cattle wealth or other movable properties like bullock cart, furniture etc. The Mahajans being very shrewd in their business, often cheated the loanee by changing the size of measurements at the time of collection. Such grievances gradually accumulated causing discontentment. Agrarian and feudal grievances drove the peasants to a breaking point in the 1930s making the situation ripe for a revolt. The man who provided leadership to the mute peasants of Mayurbhanj was Sarat Chandra Das.[22]

Sarat Chandra Das was Pleader by profession, a poet, nationalist and ardent follower of Mahatma Gandhi. As the elected Vice Chairman of Baripada Municipality, he was associated with many institutions and had rendered valuable Social service. As a close associate of Harekrushna Mahtab he had joined the Congress movement in Balasore in 1921. As the Vice President of Balasore District Congress Committee, he had gained practical experience in organisational work. He had close contact with Gopabandhu Das as well. Though a permanent resident of Baripada town, he preferred to spend much of his time at village Ambajora. For his selflessness, dedication and austere life, he was considered as the 'Gandhi of Mayurbhanj'. With great enthusiasm and uncommon zeal he gave leadership to the young nationalists of Mayurbhanj by indoctrinating them with the message of non-violence and civil disobedience propagated by Gandhiji. People loved and respected him for his 'Father Figure' and humility. From December 1938 he emerged as the undisputed leader of the people of Mayaurbhanj in their struggle for liberation from feudal oppression which was considered as the manifestation of colonialism in the Feudatory States of Orissa. Among several enthusiastic youngmen who joined the band wagon of Das, prominent ones were Gourmohan Pradhan, Dhuruva Charan Rout, Baikuntha Sadual, Jadunath Sarangi, Gangadhar Behera and Prasanna Kumar Dash. In course of time the number of followers increased and Das got ample scope to organise the peasants and activists on a sound footing.[23]

The method of political agitation in the late 1930s was quite simple. Several drummers from among the young volunteers were trained to visit the villages making announcement about the date, time and place of public meetings. They made announcement on the occasion of the weekly markets inviting the people to attend meetings in large number. Sometimes patriotic songs composed by either Sarat Chandra Das or Gourmohan Pradhan were sung to attract the attention of the people and to spread the message of Gandhiji.

Since Sarat Chandra Das was a good orator, people came in large number to his meeting in order to listen to his fiery and inspiring speeches. He could inspire many young men to join the national struggle by giving up their studies and overcoming the opposition of family members.[24]

Sarat Chandra Das was a good organiser. He laid the structural foundation of Prajamandal movement in Mayurbhanj by organising committees in each *Pargana.* Those who gave him unstinted support in organising the subaltern movement successfully were Jagannath Kamila, Giris Chandra Roy, Gourmohan Pradhan, Gajendranath Patnaik, Hrdayanath Das, Hadibandhu Rout, Govind Chandra Naik, Laxmidhar Tripathy, Sakital Soren, Ramchandra Patnaik, Laxman Parida, Dhruva Charan Rout, Krushna Charan Parida, Krushna Chandra Swain, Ramchandra Mohapatra, Madanmohan Panda, Madan Mohan Mishra, Aparti Biswal, Ramnath Patra, Biswambhar Moharana and Kilas chandra Naik.[25]

The *Pargana* Committee meetings were regularly organised to discuss the village reconstruction programme of Gandhiji which included village cleaning construction and repair of roads, raising funds through collection of rice, construction of dams for irrigation, establishment of evening Schools for the spread of literacy, formation of Co-operative societies, eradication of Caste system and untouchability and prohibition. Each Pargana Committee had a President, a Secretary, a Joint Secretary and Treasurer. All these units operated under the leadership of Sarat Chandra Das. With increasing popularity of Gandhian programme the subaltern activities could be intensified due to unity among the villagers. He made his native village Ambajora the headquarters for coordinating the activities. As pressure of work increased, he gave up his legal practice at Baripada for which his family had to face acute financial hardship. He kept close contact with eminent Congress workers at Balasore like Harekrushna Mahtab. By his own sacrifice of a flourishing legal career he could create a very good impression among the young generation of nationalists. When the subaltern activities could get a definite form and receive momentum in 1939 March-April, Das named the organisation as 'Mayurbhanj Prajamandal'. He charted out special programme for the upliftment of women so as to make their participation in the movement more purposeful. Inspiring poems were recited by Gourmohan Pradhan at public meetings extolling the role of women in the society. The Prajamandal leaders urged upon the women activists to give up *purdah* and shun social isolation. Special meetings of women volunteers were held under the leadership of Nishamani Panda, Mania Mohapatra, and Katikamani Mohapatra. They emphasised upon the point that without women participation and awareness social welfare would remain a dream. The attempt was crowned with success as more women volunteers involved themselves in the Prajamandal movement in response to the call.[26]

For the convenience of administration, Mayurbhanj State was divided into four Sub-divisions; Sadar, Kaptipada, Panchpir and Bamaghaty. The Prajamandal movement was so widespread as to embrace all the four sub-divisions. At times the leaders used to make suitable arrangements for boarding and lodging in temporary sheds. An exhibition was also organised to display agricultural and cottage industries products of the area concerned which evoked great public interest. The Prajamandal organisation was lucky to have one young and hardworking General Secretary in Prasanna Kumar Dash who had left his studies on the eve of Matriculation examination to join the band wagon of Sarat Chandra.[27] He was only 16 years of age when he was inducted by Sarat Chandra as a drummer to make announcements about public meetings in the weekly markets of the villages. His induction was in April 1939 and despite his young age he could impress upon Sarat Chandra Das as an ardent nationalist, full of steam and eager to fight for the cause of the peasants. He belonged to a Brahmin family of village Kendumundi which had been granted rent free *jagir* land by the Rajas for the contributions made by Banamali Das (grandfather of Prasanna Kumar Dash) to promote and popularise the Chhow dance. Though an agriculturist, Jagamohan Dash, the father of Prasanna Kumar Dash was a man of robust personality and jovial temperament. The expectation of the family was belied when Prasanna Kumar became a full-time activist and left his student career for good. As an alert young man he was aware of the nationalist fire sweeping the whole country. Impressed by the Gandhian thought of village reconstruction, he had organised 'Palli Sakha' in his student days to initiate social reforms. He could not achieve much success due to the opposition of the owners of *Jagir* lands including his own family members. The Bazelgette incident suddenly caught his imagination as never beforg. He raised funds to help the people of Ranpur in their distress. Attending political meetings regularly became a passion with him.[28] It did not take much time for Sarat Chandra Das to spot out the spark in Prasanna and he groomed him personally to become an ideal politician in the future. Prasanna organised numerous public meetings and made fiery speeches befitting to the time and political scenario in the state. He was straight forward, upright and dedicated, fully committed to the cause of the anti feudal movement as would be evident from the following statement he made later (in 1942) in his capacity as the General Secretary.[29]

> Instances of forced labour and illegal exactions and realisation of exorbitant rate of interest are to be met even at this advanced stage of the world and under the very

> nose of the Government. The people being igncrant and timid, this state of theirs was taken advantage of and for a paltry amount of loan, they had to pay double, triple and four folds and at last have had in many cases to part with their ancestral lands with tears in their eyes.

In his opinion, the *Sardars* and Village *Mahajans* were primarily responsible for exploiting the innocent peasants. He protested against the stringent circular No. 3 of 27 April 1925 which had deprived the common man from the basic rights like Freedom of Speech, Association and Meetings. The public meetings organised by him were platforms for making speeches against the prevailing oppression of the Durbar administration. He, while criticising the arbitrary nature of the Durbar administration called upon the withdrawal of the above mentioned Circular but in vain.[30]

With the outbreak of the Second World War and resignation tendered by the Congress Ministry in Orissa and elsewhere, the British Government adopted drastic measures to round up the nationalists in a bid to maintain law and order in the country. But so far as the feudatory States were concerned the rising tide of popular movement had reached a point of no return. In 1938, the Orissa States Enquiry Committee had been formed to record the various grievances of the people of the Garjat States.[31] The Committee consisted of Harekrushna Mahtab as the Chairman and Balbant Rai Mehta and Lalmohan Patnaik as the members. When the Committee visited Balasore to assess the situation prevailing in Mayurbhanj and Nilgiri States, a large number of Kols and Bathudis from Mayurbhanj travelled all the way on foot covering a distance of three days' journey to tender evidence on their agrarian and other problems. A Summary of their grievances is listed below.[32]

(*i*) They paid annas Two per head of cow for grazing on the pasture land.

(*ii*) They paid every month four annas per family as fuel tax.

(*iii*) For selling cows they had to pay a levy of annas four per head.

(*iv*) They paid *rasad* to state officers during camping and during *Shikar* expeditions.

(*v*) They rendered *bethi* for repairing roads, construction of School buildings and Government offices.

(*vi*) They were disallowed to take carts on pucca roads.

(*vii*) They had to pay for cutting Salwood required for agricultural implements.

(*viii*) They had to pay Chowkidari Tax varying from annas Two to annas Four.

(*ix*) Road cess at the rate of anna one per Rupee of rent was levied on them.

(*x*) They paid marriage tax ranging from annas Four to annas Eight.

(*xi*) Those who were engaged in Sericulture had to pay a cess of annas Twelve.

It was revealed that the tribals were unaware of any medical aid facilities during epidemics. Primary Schools were few and far between. The Committee felt very much concerned at the indifferent attitude of the Chief in redressing the grievances of his subjects.[33]

The growing consciousness of the people and their organised political behaviour created an alarming situation in the State. It was evident that the wind of change had started blowing. The terrifying incident of the murder of Major R.L.

Bazelgette, the Political Agent at Ranpur by the mob in January 1939 had not been forgotten. In order to counter the Prajamandal movement, the Maharaja adopted two bold measures: One was to neutralise the popular movement by creating a parallel organisation called 'Prajamangal' and the second one was to give the people a share in the State administration through representative bodies called Praja Sabhas.[34]

The Prajamangal was a state sponsored organisation headed by Harischandra Dash, the brother of the Superintendent of Police (Ram Chandra Dash). The *Sardars, Tehsildars, Sarbarakars* and many State officials were enrolled as the members. People were persuaded to join the Prajamangal organisation by withdrawing support to Prajamandal. The aim was to create confusion between the objectives of the two organisations and thereby to mislead the people. Antisocials were engaged to disturb the public meetings of Prajamandal leaders and loans were not given to those who supported Prajamandals. Prasanna Kumar Dash felt unhappy the way these anti-socials disturbed the Independence Day Celebration and prevented the Prajamandal volunteers in completing road works at Baripada. Sometimes clashes between the Prajamandal and Prajamangal workers were reported to the Police. The State administration went a step further in designating the Prajamangal as Mayurbhanj National Congress making use of the State Flag as National Flag. The meetings of the Prajamangal were designated as meetings of the Mayurbhanj Congress.[35]

The other step taken by the Maharaja was to set up Praja Sabhas in each Sub-division with elected and nominated members to share the administration. According to the Prajasabha order 1938, two thirds of the members were to be elected on the basis of adult suffrage and the remaining one third to be nominated. The Prajasabhas had the power to consider all questions effecting the well being of the people like education, health, medical relief, water supply, agriculture; communication, and general problems. The Prajasabhas had a five year term and could be dissolved by the Dewan. Their proceedings were recorded.[36] Notwithstanding its defects this was a welcome sign in the State administration as it marked a pattern of change. But Prasanna Kumar Dash, the Prajamandal Spokesman thought otherwise. According to his statement.[37]

> These Praja Sabhas are Institutions quite independent of each other and with no central body of a coordinating character. They have got no real power in them to carry any binding effect of their decisions on the executive heads of the State.

Elsewhere in other Garjat States the Prajamandals were fighting to put an end to the ruthless autocracy of the Rajas. The situation inspired the Mayurbhanj Prajamandal to fight for similar objectives despite the fact that the Raja was not that autocratic. Serious political campaigning by Bansidhar Behera and Sarat Chandra Das to draw mass support began to show results. The number of Prajamandal supporters began to swell. Like Prasanna Kumar Dash the School students in large number were drawn to the vortex of politics. The Prajasabha experiment of the chief did not find many buyers. A new wave of political consciousness similar to that of quit India movement created mass upsurge in the State. Sarat Chandra's programme of village reconstruction was warmly received in the Tribal areas. The message was carried to the people by young enthusiasts like Prasanna Kumar Dash who made the rural folks conscious of the outdated feudal practices and the significance of civil rights. He and his compatriots were not loosing patience. They simply increased the

Parganna Samities and opened new branches in the villages with more members. People joined the *Parganna Samities* with the conviction that membership would earn for them immunity from the oppression of the Sardars. The Prajamandal printed more brochures, arranged more public meetings, composed numerous patriotic songs to inspire the people for a final show down. With the participation of women, a new dimension was already created. Sarat Chandra Das' alertness kept his organisation well informed about the day to day developments in other Princely States of Orissa. Since some of his associates like Bansidhar Behera, Radha Krushna Pradhan, and Gourmohan Pradhan were veteran Congress workers, the profound influence of Indian National Congress on the Mayurbhanj Prajamandal was quite natural. It was rightly felt that the political movements in Mayurbhanj was an echo of the Congress agitation in the adjacent districts. The Prajamandal now demanded responsible and representative Government in Mayurbhanj. To appease the people, the Maharaja made an announcement on 23 April 1945 that Mayurbhanj would have a Kendra Parishad (Central Legislature) with 27 members, including 15 nominated members to function as an Advisory body for a period of three years. A draft constitution was laid down. It stipulated that the Parishad would have the right of making laws for all persons, all courts, all places and things in Mayurbhanj. A bill passed by the Parishad would have the force of an Act after it received the assent of the Maharaja.[39]

According to the provisions of the Constitution, the first election to the Mayurbhanj Kendra Parishad was held on 10 January 1946 marking an important stage in the political development of the State. It was evident that the Maharaja tried to involve his people in State administration to diffuse the growing tension. He also appointed a Committee to suggest measures for the formation of village Panchayats.

Since the creation of village Panchayats was an objective of Gandhian movement and the Prajamandals, the steps taken by the Maharaja was aimed at taking the wind away from the sail of Prajamandal movement. Therefore, the Prajamandal leaders were not feeling appeased. The struggle for a popular Government in Mayurbhanj continued unabated. More public meetings were organised to expedite the process of change from monarchy to democracy.[40]

A very grave situation occurred in February 1947 when Paiks under the leadership of Baikuntha Nath Sadual rose in rebellion as a protest against the abolition of *Jagir* land. The disturbance led to the arrest and conviction of Sadual. The incident further aggravated the political crisis in the State. At this juncture, the Regional Council of Orissa and Chhatisgarh States peoples was setup under the Chairmanship of Sarangdhar Das. Three members in the Executive Committee were from Mayurbhanj Prajamandal. Prasanna Kumar Dash was elected as one of the Joint Secretaries. Already the conference at Pratappur held in July 1947 had passed a resolution for a final confrontation with the State authorities by taking a large procession to Baripada on 15 August 1947. At other places the Prajamandal movement reached the highest crescendo expecting the Durbar administration to fall on 15 August 1947 simultaneously with the transfer of power by the British Government to Indian National Congress. The Prajamandal members of the Mayurbhanj Kendra Parishad submitted their resignation. An Action Committee consisting of Sarat Chandra Das, Prasanna Kumar Dash, Harihar Mohanty, Gourmohan Pradhan, Bhaktabandhu Mohanta and Ananta Rath submitted a charter of demands on 30 June 1947 urging upon the Maharaja for the expeditious establishment of a responsible Government in Mayurbhanj.[41] They intensified their agitation and called upon the Maharaja to concede to their demands by 16 September 1947.

Disillusioned by the development; the Maharaja dissolved the Kendra Parishad on 7 July 1947 and opened negotiation with the leaders for a peaceful solution of the crisis. He had no desire to take any ruthless steps against the *Satyagrahis*. The negotiation resulted in a settlement. It was decided that the Prajamandal would furnish a list of members to function as an Interim Government and the State would become an independent unit of Indian union with the Maharaja discharging the functions of a constitutional monarch.[42]

The members of the cabinet of the interim Government were nominated by the Maharaja on 9 December 1947. They were also allotted with portfolios as under:

(*i*) Sarat Chandra Das, Premier

Portfolios: Home, Finance, Audit, Planning and Reconstruction.

(*ii*) Bidyadhar Mahapatra, Minister

Portfolios: Revenue, Law, Health and Local Government.

(*iii*) Mahesvar Naik, Minister

Portfolios: Development, Education, supply, Transport, Public Works, Commerce and Labour.

Transfer of power took place on 10 December 1947.[43] The day was declared a Public holiday on account of the victory of the Prajamandal in peacefully accomplishing the task of having a popular Government installed in place of feudal aristocracy. Mayurbhanj was the first Princely state in India to have achieved such a great success. A Constituent Assembly was setup simultaneously to frame a constitution. It was indeed a landmark in the history of Prajamandal movement. Sarat Chandra Das received warm and congratulatory greetings from the Congress leaders like Dr.

Rajendra Prasad and Jawaharlal Nehru for his victory in a struggle against the feudal social order and outdated monarchical Government. It was an occasion for gala celebration.[44]

But the euphoria of popular victory did not last long. Though it was a unique experiment for the Prajamandal leaders of Mayurbhanj their lack of administrative experience was a burdensome liability. They conducted the State administration for approximately eleven months with some creditable achievements. The abolition of *Paik Jagir* and *Sardari* System without paying compensation spoke well of their noble principles. By completing the irrigation project at Silaghati the popular Government added another feather to its cap. All feudal levies like *Payeka Pancha, bethi, rasad* etc. were abolished. A Degree College was established at Baripada meeting thereby a longfelt desideratum in the sphere of higher education. In order to spread literacy among the adults as many as 174 Night Schools were opened. Adhering to the Gandhian principle of Prohibition the Government introduced necessary executive order for the purpose but found it very difficult to implement effectively. The reason for the failure of the Prohibition policy may be attributed to the tribal composition of the people in the State.[45]

However various factors led to the fall of the popular Government of Sarat Chandra Das. There was a mounting pressure to merge Mayurbhanj with Bihar.[46] A tribal uprising was an imminent threat to law and order. The Maharaja and Sarat Chandra Das wisely met Sardar Patel and V.P. Menon in New Delhi to sign the merger documents and handed over the State administration to the Central Government on 16 October 1948.[47] For two and half months the state was administered by the Government of India through Mr. Rege, I.C.S the Commissioner. Under his strong administration the tribal uprising was crushed. On 1 January 1949 Mayurbhanj merged with Orissa and was constituted a district. Necessary changes were introduced for its administrative integration with the Province. The Government press was handed over to the Utkal University. Since the University was passing through a difficult period on account of financial crunch the State Bank of Mayurbhanj donated Rupees Eight lakhs to the University to tide over the crisis. The Research Section of the Jubilee Library with its precious books and Journals was transferred to the Orissa State Museum, Bhubaneswar.[48]

Prasanna Kumar Dash was a force to reckon with in the period when Sarat Chandra Das was the Premier of Mayurbhanj. He was the alter ego of the latter, and a constant companion of his mentor all through his political career.[49] At the time of merger with Orissa Biswanath Das was the President of Utkal Pradesh Congress Committee. He allowed the leaders of both Prajamandal and Prajamangal parties to join the Congress which displeased the Prajamandal leaders. They were victims of the Pro-feudal Prajamangal party of Mayurbhanj which had supported Darbar administration. Therefore, equal treatment accorded by the President of the Pradesh Congress Committee to the Prajamangal leaders was an unfortunate experience for Sarat Chandra Das and his colleagues. Such humiliation meted out to the erstwhile Prajamandal leaders of Mayurbhanj being intolerable Sarat Chandra and Prasanna Kumar had to take some independent decisions. In order to maintain self dignity they finally dissociated themselves from the Congress organisation and turned to Socialism as the goal of their political career.[50] Almost all Prajamandal workers resigned from the Congress to join the Orissa Samajbadi Dal (Socialist Party) under the leadership of Surendra Nath Dwibedy. Sarat Chandra Das took retirement from politics soon afterwards on account of physical illness.

References

1. L.E.B. Cobden Ramsay, *Feudatory States of Orissa,* (Reprint, 1982). These states were Athgarh, Athmallik, Bamra, Baramba, Baud, Bonai, Daspalla, Dhenkanal, Gangpur, Hindol, Kalahandi, Keonjhar, Khandpara, Mayurbhanj, Narsinghpur, Nayagarh, Nilgiri, Pallahara, Patna-Balangir, Rairakhol, Ranpur, Sonepur, Talcher, Tigiria, Sareikela and Kharswan.

   Area of Mayurbhanj 6365 Sq.K, Ms. (For other Statistics See pp. 236-42).
2. D.M. Praharaj, *Tribal Movements and Plitical History of India,* (New Delhi, 1986), pp. 77-80.
3. *Ibid.,* pp. 80-84.
5. *Ibid.*, pp. 85-88.
6. *Ibid.*, pp. 129-43.
7. Prasanna Kumar Dash, *A Short History of Liberation Movement in Mayurbhanj* (Oriya) (Cuttack, 1987), p. 8.
8. Sadasiba Pradhan, *Agrarian and Political Movements,* (New Delhi, 1986), pp. 155-66.
9. D.M. Praharaj, *op. cit.*, p. 119.
10. Circular No. 3 dated 27 April, 1925. Report on the Administration of Mayurbhanj (RAM) 1938-39, p. 6.
11. Prasanna Kumar Dash, *op. cit.*, p. 11.
12. *Ibid.*
13. *Ibid.*, pp. 11-13.
14. *Ibid.*, p. 13.
15. *Ibid.*, p. 14.
16. All India States Peoples Conference, (Nehru Museum & Library) (Hereafter AISPC) File No. 128, p. 113.
17. *Desa Sevak,* p. 30; and B. Mohanty, *Panchpir Praja Mandala Itihas* (Oriya, 1978), p. 1.
18. D.M. Praharaj, *op. cit.,* pp. 130-131.
19. *Ibid.*

20. *Ibid.*
21. *Ibid.*
22. *Ibid.*, p. 195.
23. Prasanna Kumar Dash, *op. cit.*, p., 14.
24. *Ibid.*, pp. 15-17.
25. For details See *Ibid.*, pp. 15-22.
26. *Ibid.*, pp. 23-25.
27. Prasanna Kumar Dash *Autobiography* in Oriya, Cuttack, 1996, pp. 8-9.
28. *Ibid.*, pp. 1-3. Major Bazelegette was the British Political Agent of Orissa Feudatory States who was killed brutally by the mob of Rampur State.
29. *Orissa History Congress Sourenir*, Special Issue on Mayurbhanj, 1982, Baripada, p. 1.
30. *Ibid.*
31. Sadasiba Pradhan, *op. cit.*, pp. 93-96. The Orissa States People Conference was formed on 20 June, 1931. It was a Provincial unit of the All India States Peoples Conference founded by Congress leaders like Balwantrai Mehta, Manilal Kothari, and G.R. Abhyankar. It had been setup in December 1927. (A.N. Sundari Sanou, *Indian States Register and Directory* (Madras, 1929), pp. 301-16). Its objective was to initiate necessary reforms in the administration of the States by the force of collective opinion of the people. Apart from demanding *Swarajya,* the Conference urged for the separation of the State revenue from the personal expenditure of the Ruler and demanded an independent Judiciary separate from the Executive.
32. Report of the Enquiry Committee, 1929, pp. 54-57.
33. *Ibid.*
34. *Annual Report, Mayurbhanj* (Hereafter RAM) *RAM*, 1938-39, p. 8.
35. AISPC (NML) File No. 128, P. 53; Also See Prasanna Kumar Dash, *op. cit.* (1987), pp. 31-37.
36. *RAM* 1938-39, p. 7; Extraordinary States Gazette, 23 November 1938.

37. AISPC (NMML) file No. 128, p. 111.
38. Prasanna Kumar Dash, *op. cit.*, 1987, pp. 38-39.
39. *Mayurbhanj State Gazette,* 23 April 1945 and *RAM*, 1945-46, Introduction.
40. Prasanna Kumar Dash, *op. cit.*, 1987, pp. 51-52.
41. *Ibid.*, pp. 53-54.
42. *Extraordinary Mayurbhanj State Gazette,* 10 December 1947.
43. *Ibid.*, 13 December 1947.
44. Sadasiba Pradhan, *op. cit.*, p. 186.
45. Prasanna Kumar Dash, *op. cit.,* 1987, pp. 57-58.
46. D. M. Praharaj, *op. cit.,* pp. 158-159.
47. N. Senapati (ed.), *Orissa District Gazetteers Mayurbhanj* 1967, p. 83. Extraordinary Mayurbhanj State Gazette, 10 November, 1948.
48. Prasanna Kumar Dash, *op. cit.,* 1987, p. 58 and D.M. Praharaj, *op. cit.,* pp. 157-58.
49. Prasanna Kumar Dash, *Autobiography, op. cit.*, See Preface.
50. The matter has been elaborately discussed in the above mentioned *Autobiography.* See pp. 55-56.

2

Decades of Destiny

Since the moment Prajamandal leaders of Mayurbhanj handed over some assets of the State administration to Harekrushna Mahtab at the Inspection Bungalow at Bhadrak[1] the stark realities of merger loomed large over their political future. For Mahtab, the prospect of accession of Mayurbhanj with Orissa was a crowning success of his political career. He not only completed the process of merger of the Feudatory States with Orissa Province, but also claimed for himself the pride of being recognised as the 'maker of modern Orissa'.[2] But for Sarat Chandra Das and his associates, the event was an anti climax. With the merger of Mayurbhanj Prajamandal with the Provincial Congress organisation, the leadership was shifted to Cuttack. Mahtab not only absorbed the Prajamandal leaders in the Congress party, he also kept the door of Congress membership open to the Prajamangal leaders of Mayurbhanj who had ceaselessly supported the feudal aristocracy and opposed Sarat Chandra Das tooth and nail by various methods in the Darbar period. Persons like Haris Chandra Dash and Ratikanta Patnaik were political adversaries of Sarat Chandra Das. They had adopted various strategies to foil the constructive programme of the Prajamandal organisation. Alongwith such sinister characters, many other opportunists joined the Provincial Congress organisation much to the chagrin of Sarat Chandra Das. The growing dissatisfaction in the Prajamandal camp became evident when Sarat Chandra Das succumbed to the rude shock. After withdrawing himself from active politics, he fell ill and breathed his last.[3] His compatriots withdrew from the Congress organisation to join the Socialist Party. This not only happened in Mayurbhanj, but also throughout the country. It was an All-India phenomenon when longtime Congress leaders decided to adopt a new political course. What happened in Mayurbhanj was a mere echo of the All-India event.[4]

Soon after his release from prison in 1946 the renowned Socialist leader Jay Prakash Narayan expressed his desire to reorganise the Congress Socialist Party. He wrote:

> The official policy of the Congress today is not a policy of struggle or preparation of a struggle; it is rather a policy of compromise and constitutionalism. Therefore, it is not possible for those of us today who still adhere to the policy of struggle and revolutionary action to function in the name of the Congress. [5]

At the All-India convention held at Kanpur from 24 February to 2 March 1947 under the Chairmanship of Rammanohar Lohia, it was decided that the Congress Socialists were unhappy at the proposed decision of the Indian National Congress leaders to partition the country on communal basis. There was an apprehension that the British Government wanted to dismember India by transferring power to the native Princes with whom they had separate Treaties and Engagements. The Socialists were aware of the declining influence of Gandhiji on the Congress Party. They therefore, resolved to organise the farmers, the workers, the Prajamandals and other like-minded people to launch a

Socialist movement. They changed the name of the Congress Socialist Party to Socialist Party and invited Congress workers to join the same. They took special interest to propagate their aims and programmes in the princely states where the peasants under the banner of Prajamandal were already on an agitational course. Several party branches were setup in these princely states. The Socialist Party had leaders like Jaya Prakash, Dr. Lohia, Acharya Narendra Dev and Ashok Mehta with great clout in the national forum. In Orissa, Sarangdhar Das and Damodar Swarup Seth were the early members.[6]

The Orissa branch of the Congress Socialist Party was set up on 28 October 1946 with the following office bearers.

Surendra Nath Dwivedy, General Secretary

Rabindra Mohan Das, Acting General Secretary

Bankabehari Das, Organisational Secretary

Gourchandra Das, Rabi Ghosh and Nishamani Khuntia as members of the executive body.[7]

They had fully endorsed the resolution passed at Nagpur convention (from 29 to 31 August 1947). They agreed with Acharya Narendra Deva's statement that the Indian National Congress was incapable of achieving socialism and it would be appropriate to leave the Congress on account of differences in principle. In order to create an embarrassing situation for the Congress, the Socialists harped on three basic issues of differences, viz, (1) Congress to clearly declare its commitment to the establishment of a Socialist Society in India; (2) Mass organisation of the youth, farmers, workers, professionals and middle-class should be formed; and (3) These organisations should be affiliated to the main body of the Congress organisation. This step was taken by the Socialists to pave their way of separation from the Congress party. Since the Indian National Congress was squarely held responsible for the partition of India and creation of Pakistan, the Socialists felt that the moment of divide had come and they were unwilling to remain in the Congress.[8]

Another issue which widened the rift in the Congress organisation was the question of finding out a substitute for Acharya Kripalani when he resigned from the Presidentship in 1947. Since most of the top leaders were members in the Cabinet of Jawaharlal Nehru, Gandhiji proposed the names of Acharya Narendra Deva and Jaya Prakash Narayan. The suggestion was vehemently opposed by Sardar Patel and his group as they did not like to give such an important post to the Socialists. They adopted a hardliner attitude to the Socialists and wished that no Socialist should get elected to the All India Congress Committee.

In Orissa, Harekrushna Mahtab exercised full control over the Congress organisation. Whosoever differed from him had to quit the party. It was at his behest the members of the Prajamangal in Mayurbhanj were admitted to the Congress organisation. The Prajamandal leaders were either required to agree with his way of doing things or get out of the Congress. In the situation those who had Socialistic leanings or connections with the Socialist Party were to decide whether to give up Congress ideology or Socialism.[9] Many of them realised that to work for Socialism by staying in the Congress Party was not possible. So finally, on 28 October 1946, the Orissa branch of the Socialist Party was setup with Surendra Nath Dwivedy as the General Secretary. Those who had worked for the peasants welfare in the Prajamandal organisation were happy to join the Socialist Party. They had no temptation to enjoy power or political clout. Initially, the Party was faced with financial problem and the opposition of Mahtab. But the members were a dedicated lot. As messengers of Socialism they worked with great zeal and courage. Their main aim was to establish democratic socialism which was quite different from Marxian Communism. They wanted power to be transferred to the Indian masses. They envisaged popular revolution. Explaining the goal, a brochure published by the Orissa Socialist Party stated.

> In order to realise the objective of a peasant-worker State, as a first step, we should have to create a powerful mass organisation in order to ensure that the British Government indeed gets out of India by June 1948. Not only that, in addition to the elimination of British rule in India, we want that the land belonging to the Zamindars should be taken over by the Krushak Panchayats in the villages; the workers should take over the ownership of the factories, and the state peoples should take over the administration. These were the urgent tasks before us. If we could achieve all that by June 1948 then we should have laid a solid foundation of socialism.[10]

The Socialists abhorred the idea of joining the Constituent Assembly of India. They remained busy building up mass organisations among the peasants, workers, youth etc. outside the Congress. A Press setup by them at Cuttack was known as the Krushak Press which revived the weekly publication 'Krushak'. Many branches of the Krushak Sangha were setup in Orissa. In the Conferences organised by them, the participants discussed about the problems of the share croppers. These efforts gave new dimension and vigour to the Prajamandal movement which was gradually loosing its impact. The weekly 'Krushak' served as the mouthpiece of the rural peasants and their problems.

To organise the students and youth, the Samajvadi Yuvak Sabha was setup. For the young people the Lok Seva Dal was started to impart physical training and to inculcate mass discipline. A cultural organisation called the Jana Sanskruti Sangha was formed to generate interest in culture and nationalism. These programmes of social reconstruction caught the imagination of people like Prasanna Kumar Das who plunged headlong to the Socialist movement in 1949 alongwith Giris Chandra Roy, Gourmohan Pradhan and others. They had no other choice. After the death of Gandhiji on 30 January 1948, the Congress Party increasingly became autocratic. It not only drifted away from the principle of democratic socialism, but also disallowed any constructive criticism inside the organisation. Gandhiji's suggestion to dissolve the Congress and replace it by a Lok Sevak Sangha fell into deaf ears. The words of Acharya Narendra Deva provided the moral force to the Socialists to leave Congress Party. In 1948 he observed,

> It is not that we are in a hurry to quit the Congress. The Congress is compelling us to get out of it. xxx By one door the Congress expels the Socialists. Through another, it admits in capitalists and communalists. God alone can save the Congress. We are not coming out of the Congress with broken hearts. Our ideals are different. There exists today ideological incompatibility. There are signs that the Government are becoming totalitarian. Authoritarianism is growing in the Congress. There is a demand for a democratic, free, fearless and healthy opposition to the party in power. The Socialist Party alone can fulfil this demand. It is a challenge of history and we must accept it.[11]

The decision to quit the Congress Party was taken in a public meeting at Baripada in September 1949. The leadership was taken over by Prasanna Kumar Dash. A brochure published in Oriya was circulated explaining the reasons of leaving the Congress party. It was a very painful exercise for the veteran Prajamandal leaders of Mayurbhanj . The Congress leadership in Orissa did not distinguish between the Prajamandal and Prajamangal. Advertently, they humiliated the Prajamandal leaders by giving recognition to those (like

Harischandra Dash, Ratikanta Patnaik etc.) who were staunch opponents of democratic movement. The Socialist leaders like Surendra Nath Dwibedy, Rabindra Mohan Das, Sarangdhar Das and Bankabehari Das welcomed the disillusioned leaders of Mayurbhanj to their newly formed Party. Prasanna Kumar Dash immediately undertook the strenuous work of spreading Socialist ideology in the subdivisions of Mayurbhanj.[12] He became the President of the Peasants Organisation in Mayurbhanj with Giris Chandra Roy as the Secretary. For the good works he did to focus upon the problems of the Share Croppers, Prasanna Kumar was nominated to the Executive Committee of the Provincial body. Later on he became a permanent member of the Executive Committee.

The visit of Jaya Prakash Narayan to Mayurbhanj and the series of public meetings addressed by him provided great impetus to the swelling tide of Socialism. In each Police Station an unit of the Socialist Party was formed to organise the peasants as a solid base for social changes. In 1950 Ashok Mehta was another all-India Socialist leader to visit Mayurbhanj. This helped in strengthening the Socialist movement at the grass root level.

The first General election on the basis of universal adult franchise was held in 1952. Ten seats were allotted to Mayurbhanj for representation in the Orissa Legislative Assembly with seven reserved and three General constituencies. The Socialist Party decided to put Girischandra Roy and Prasanna Kumar Das as party candidates from Baripada and Muruda constituency respectively. Although for filing nomination and campaigning for election was not a very expensive affair, both the above candidates were in positive disadvantage for lack of funds and conveyance. The election was fought with great austerity. Prasanna Kumar Das had to move on bicycle and bullock cart to reach the voters in scattered villages. His main contestant was Kamini Kanta Patnaik, the son of Ratikanta Patnaik, a former *Sardar* and influential person of Muruda. Yet he was assured of all support by Naba Krushna Choudhury, the Chief Minister on condition that he would rejoin the Congress after election. The Chief Minister also promised to take care of Muruda constituency if his condition would be accepted by Dash. But as changing the party was against his moral principle, Dash politely declined the offer of the Chief Minister and campaigned for the election on his own merit. He got elected to the Assembly with a lead of about three thousand votes than his nearest rival. Giris Chandra Roy also got elected from Baripada constituency. That four candidates of the Socialist Party got elected to the Legislative Assembly was no mean achievement.

The Socialists played the role of constructive opposition in the Orissa Legislative Assembly for almost two decades until its dissolution in 1971. The emergence of Indira Gandhi in Indian politics with her 'Garibi hatao' programme and nationalisation of the Banks etc. gave a new look to the Indian National Congress. In the General Election of 1971 the Congress Party had a landslide victory all over the country at the cost of minor and regional parties. For the Socialists, the 1971 election administered a rude shock. Its existence was found to be in jeopardy. Internal dissension was another cause for its dissolution. Indira Gandhi evinced an interest to admit the erstwhile Socialists to the Congress Party to bolster her political image. On her invitation, the Socialists of Orissa like Prasanna Kumar Dash, Nishamani Khuntia, Bankabehari Das, and Bhagabat Prasad Mohanty etc. jointed the Indian National Congress. But when the Nandini Satpathy Ministry was formed in 1972, though there was speculation that Prasanna Kumar Dash would be inducted as a Minister, he declined to be sworn in for two reasons. Firstly, the Socialists had an understanding among themselves to project Banka Behari Das as a prospective minister. Secondly, since he was not elected to the Assembly with a ticket of the Congress Party, he felt it would be unethical to assume ministership in the Congress led Government. That Satpathy's ministry failed to survive as a stable Government was a different issue. For that the internal feud among the politicians of Orissa and their self interest contributed substantially.[13] The internecine conflict finally led to the imposition of Governor's rule for one year which further frustrated the expectations of ambitious persons.

During 1952 to 1972 the role of Prasanna Kumar Dash on the floor of the Assembly need proper study. He was elected as many as five times to the State Legislature notwithstanding the fact that he could not nourish his constituency as he should have. Being in the opposition his role was always to analyse and criticise the policies of the Government keeping the larger interest of the people in mind. He never dreamt to be in the Treasury benches. Sitting in the opposition party, he assisted the Leader Nishamani Khuntia and acted as the whip of the Socialist Party. Although the members were paid Rs. 150 as pay per mensem and Rupees Ten per day as daily allowance, obeying party discipline he received Rupees Forty only per month for his maintenance. The rest was spent for the party. Each member was required to recruit two peasants to the party annually. The Party leadership expected the members to play the role of responsible legislator. Since there were only four Socialist members each had his specific responsibility and department to look after. None was experienced in legislative business. Therefore, they had to learn the ABC of legislative procedure from veteran members. What was a budget, how to introduce it, what was adjournment motion, how to put Questions and Supplementaries etc. were unknown and had to be properly understood for success in the House. As members of the Shadow Cabinet they often discussed matters of public importance among themselves. Since Prasanna Kumar Dash was to take care of Forest Department, he was satirically referred to as an Expert on Forest. He played his role sincerely and well drawing the appreciation of all.

In the all-India Conference of the Socialists, Prasanna Kumar Dash represented Orissa first at Allahabad and later at Gwalior and Nagpur. He made Socialism in Mayurbhanj a force to reckon with. His efforts to protect the interest of the Share Croppers was crowned with success. The pro-peasant attitude of Nabakrushna Choudhury, the Chief Minister of Orissa was a positive support to Dash in his struggle for the rights of the Share Croppers against the exploiting landlords of Baisinga. [24]

As a member of the Orissa Legislative Assembly he participated in the debate on Minor Irrigation Scheme and their need for an agricultural community.[15] He did not support the private monopoly of Kenduleaf business. He was utterly unhappy with the arbitrary manner in which the Government officers were behaving in Mayurbhanj after its merger with Orissa. Since the Service conditions of the ex-State employees stipulated sixty years of age for superannuation, he pleaded for its observation in letters and spirit.[16]

Since the Provincial Government had presented a deficit budget, Dash opposed the enlargement of Council of Ministers.[17] He further suggested a drastic cut in the privy purse of the former rulers of Garjat States.[18] In his considered opinion the sum ear-marked for payment of Privy purse, should better be utilised in the general welfare of the public or in exploiting mineral wealth of the State.[19] The Education budget required higher budgetary allocation, he said.[20] The State of affairs in Mayurbhanj always received priority attention of Dash. He lamented the fast depletion of forest wealth and pleaded for more funds to rejuvenate the Spinning and Weaving Mills of Mayurbhanj. The prospecting of venadium mines in Bamanghaty Subdivision was another priority area on which he focussed his attention.[21]

With great concern for agriculture, Prasanna Kumar Dash explained the impact of forest on rain and agricultural production. Since the forests were being destroyed by unscrupulous contractors he cautioned the Government to take preventive measures.[22] Protection of forests and prevention of illegal felling of trees became the focal point of his debate again and again.[23] He urged upon the Government to nationalise Kenduleaf trade so that the prevailing exploitation of the innocent tribals could be stopped. He proposed a novel idea of constituting District Committees to ensure improvement in agriculture.[24] As a staunch Socialist he firmly believed in austerity measures in public expenses by the Government. He did not agree to enhance the pay and allowances of the Ministers in view of low pay scale of most employees in the Government.[25]

During the vote of thanks on the address of Governor, Dash got an opportunity to vehemently criticise the prevailing corruption in the administration.[26] He was in favour of decentralisation of powers. As a true follower of Gandhian ideology, he wanted the Gram Panchayats to be endowed with more powers and responsibilities.[27] He was eager to improve the lot of the rural population for which redistribution of agricultural land was considered essential. In his opinion no landlord should be allowed to keep cultivable land unutilised. The law should provide adequate protection to the share croppers. This was emphasised upon because the Government wanted to extend the life of the Tenancy Protection Act, 1948, by a couple of years more.[28]

Dash gave a very thought provoking speech when the Demand for Forest Department came for voting. In his opinion the forest wealth provided a source of revenue for the State. But the annual revenue was showing a downward trend due to consistent destruction of forest wealth. He observed that the contractors deliberately kept bidding at a low rate and expenditure of the Department was increasing. He lamented over the fact that the administration of the department was not organisaed a commercial basis. Neither the Forest lands had been clearly demarcated, nor care was taken to prevent illegal felling of trees. He wished the activities of the working Plan Division and Forest utilisation Department to be properly coordinated. He was unhappy over the negligence shown on plantation/afforesation and indifferent attitude in dealing with the migratory tribes. Not only the Contractors were a source of danger to Forest wealth, the Saw Mill owners and paper mill owners were equally dangerous for causing severe damage to Forests.[29] The debate showed his genuine concern over the issue.

When the Government sought the cooperation of the Assembly on the Appropriation Bill, Dash came down heavily on the makers of the Budget for not foreseeing things in time. If the Government was failing to utilise budgetary allocation, how would they execute the Five Year Plans, Dash asked. He felt concerned over the fact that the Government was indifferent to infrastructural development before undertaking industrialisation in a large scale. He was right to point out that without power there could be no Industrial growth.[30]

Educational growth of Orissa was another major issue for which Dash felt worried. The Government was planning to have a Board of Secondary Education free from the existing system of University control. To have uniformity and quality in Secondary education, he proposed all Secondary Schools to be brought under Government management. And education should have greater relevance to the society was his view point. He spoke of universal education too.[31]

Likewise, the Anchal Sasan bill which aimed at decentralisation of administration was whole heartedly supported by him. In his opinion, power to govern should rest on the people. That way the foundation of democracy could be strengthened. The Local Self Government should deal with education and agriculture. This would ensure proper welfare of the community. According to the Anchal Sasan Bill objectives, it was stipulated,

> the present bill seeks to give full shape to his plan of setting up a local authority at a level higher than the Gram Panchayats so that peoples representatives may have a decisive voice in conducting activities in the fields of public health, education, agriculture, development of cottage industries, etc. that directly concern their welfare.[32]

Responding to the feelings of the Assembly, the Governor in his annual speech stated,

> It is the policy of my Government to gradually entrust to the Panchayats more and more responsibility for the execution of local works of development.[33]

Dash insisted upon further decentralisation of powers for the success of Indian democracy. He pleaded for democratic socialism. He did not want the powers to remain with the bureaucrats because such colonial tradition was against popular interest as envisaged in Gandhian programme. People alone could implement the objectives of planning. He, therefore, suggested that Minor Irrigation projects, veterinary and agriculture be handled by the Gram Panchayats.[34]

While discussing the budget demand on Forest, Dash got an opportunity to expose the mismanagement in the

Department. He criticised the non-availability of a status report on the functioning of the Department. In his opinion protection of Forest should be given Top Priority in the working agenda. Forest is the source of human civilisation, he observed. But due to erosion of soil the abode of serenity and meditation would be destroyed soon. Since 28% of Orissa's land mass is covered by forest, the efficient management of the natural resources would be a rich source of income for the state. He expressed his displeasure in the absence of a uniform system of rules governing forest of the coastal districts and the Garjat States. He was against allowing any human habitation in the forest areas. He would not permit any *podhu* cultivation to destroy the virgin forest. To improve efficiency of the Department he suggested a thorough reorganisation of the Range/Division and circle besides classifying the jungles. To ward off destructive agencies he proposed powers be vested on the Gram Panchayats. In order to utilise the services of the staff, he advised the Government to impart training of plantation among the Forest Guards. In his opinion afforesation was most essential to preserve the forest wealth.[35]

Like the management of forests, the Mining Department attracted the attention of vigilant Dash. He not only considered the desirability of creating a separate department of Mining, but also suggested the leadership should be entrusted to a Technical person. He painfully noted the lack of planning in exploiting the rich mineral resources of the State and also observed the advantages enjoyed by the unscrupulous lease holders. The state was losing royalty and rare minerals were being exported to outside. Due to the absence of a Mining School in Orissa, the State was deprived of technical personnel to handle its rich mineral wealth. The prevalence of corruption and nepotism at every sphere of administration worried him too much.[36]

Coming to the labour problem, particularly that of agricultural labourers in Orissa, Dash proposed that the problem could be approached from two sides: (*i*) the welfare of the working class, and (*ii*) the economic stability and progress of the province. He urged upon the Government to fulfil the basic needs of the workers like food, clothing and shelter. He was in favour of providing the workers with improved medical facilities, better educational opportunities, social security and increased secretarial facilities. He insisted upon sincere implementation of workers' Insurance. He found out that the plight of the agricultural labourers was much worse than the industrial workers. The remedy was in a change of attitude, he said.[37]

The Swadeshi spirit in Dash made him to participate in the discussion centring the Official Language Bill, 1954. He supported the bill because he was convinced that the society as a whole was tending towards English culture in dress, address, language and attitude. To him English language evoked fear, respect and curiosity. Though, English language was a passport to expeditious disposal, he did not consider it beneficial for the country.[38]

There was a draught situation in the northern districts of Orissa in 1954 which warranted immediate relief measures. It was suggested by Dash that District Food Committees be formed in the scarcity areas. He also suggested project works to provide employment to agriculture labourers. [39] The Orissa Sales Tax (Amendment) Bill, 1954 came for discussion. Dash made a comparative analysis of Orissa Sales Tax with Income Tax and pointed out many defects in Orissa Sales Tax in order to make it more humane and equitable. He urged upon the Government for quick disposal of cases to help the traders.[40]

The prevailing corruption in various spheres of the administration was like a bug-bear for Dash. He suggested the setting up a Tribunal to remove corruption from Police Department. He lamented over the callous attitude of the Government to check corruption and resultant injury caused to the citizens.[41]

As a staunch Socialist, Dash was keen for the introduction of land reforms. He would appreciate the creation of a Land Tribunal to give expeditious justice to the farmers. He did not find the Tenants Protection Act as adequate safeguard. He observed that the Government was not eager to introduce reforms and the Land Tenure Committees set up for the purpose were not working.

As the Demand on Forest Department was tabled for voting, Dash raised several pertinent issues. He was not supporting the demand since no steps had been taken to improve the forests. All plannings had failed creating acute scarcity of an essential item like firewood. The department had not only failed to demarcate the forest lands, but also to protect the existing forests. The budgetary allocation seemed to be inadequate,. He wished proper coordination between the Soil Conservation, Agriculture and Forest Departments. He criticised the over centralisation in Forest administration. In view of the lackadaisical attitude of the Government, he very much wanted the Gram Panchayats to be handed over the responsibility.[42]

When the Government brought forward the Orissa Appropriation Bill (2), 1955, the voice of Dash got full throat release. He drew the attention of the House to the fact that the Government was unable to utilise the natural wealth of the State to earn revenue. High quality iron ore was not taken full advantage of. The middlemen earned more profit in Orissa than the Government. To reinforce his point he read out from the Report of the Planning Commission:

> There is large wastage, especially in minerals of marginal grades, as these are either abandoned in the mines or thrown away on the mine dumps. Ways and means must be devised for the mining and recovery of these low grade materials.

To increase state revenue, Dash suggested an upward revision of royalty.[43]

During the discussion on Orissa Tenants Relief Bill, 1955 Dash again called upon the Government to bring land reforms in the interest of the share croppers. He said,

> It is essential that pending introduction of comprehensive land reforms, statutory protection should be afforded temporarily to all tenants in actual cultivation of land.

He did not like the eviction of share croppers and to that effect insisted upon an assurance from the Speaker. He was whole heartedly sympathetic to the cause of the share croppers. Since land was the major social-economic asset of Orissa sustaining 80% population, his voice was fraught with real concern and sympathy.[44] He pleaded for improvement of agriculture and rapid industrialisation while discussing the Orissa Betterment Charges Bill, 1954. He supported the Orissa Khadi and village and Cottage Industries Board Bill, 1955 as there was scope to increase production and national wealth.[45]

When the Government solicited house approval for the Supplementary demands for Grants on Home (Police) Dash opposed the move saying that the Police attitude in a free country should change so that Police atrocities are stopped and there would be no infringement of the liberty of the people. Referring to the recent incidents of States Reorganisation Commission Movement he cited instances of police molesting women and causing physical harm to men.[46]

There was a marathon debate on the Second Five Year Plan in April 1956. The discussion centred round the principle of Socialistic pattern of society. Dash wanted to know if the Government had made an assessment of their achievements during the First Five Year Plan. The increase in GDP rate was quite insignificant, he observed. Since in the First Five Year Plan there was more allocation on Agriculture did it show encouraging result in promoting the economic condition of the peasants, he asked . In his opinion, India being primarily an agricultural country, the shifting of priorities was ominous. To him the statements made by the Congress leaders appeared controversial. The Government should control both production and distribution and ensure better facilities of education, health and employment for all. He favoured the nationalisation of Industries and Banks. There should be no disparity in the Salary structure of the employees. He could not appreciate in full the strange concept of mixed economy about which the Government was so vociferous. He pleaded for giving the workers a share in the management of Industries. Planning was not merely to spend the allotted amount but spending it well and properly, he said. In his opinion the Government policy of entrusting the District Magistrate, Subdivisional officer and the Block Development officer with the entire responsibility of Plan implementation was faulty.[47]

Dash had an abiding interest in the rich heritage of Orissan culture. As soon as the Orissa Ancient Monuments Preservation Bill, 1956 was tabled before the Assembly, he tried to convince the House, the efficacy of proper survey and documentation of ancient monuments. He had realised the importance of having good roads and communication facilities to the ancient sites of historical importance. Citing the example of Khiching in Mayurbhanj he appreciated the conservation work done by the State administration before independence. He admired the revival of an ancient craft of stone carving which could provide livelihood to several hundred families in the adjacent villages.[48]

As an erstwhile organiser of the Prajamandal movement in Mayurbhanj, Dash had earned the reputation of antifedual and Pro-Peasant leanings. Therefore, he welcomed the Orissa Estates Abolition (Second Amendment) Bill in 1956. The Bill proposed the abolition of Landlordism and feudal social structure. He fervently desired the Government to take expeditious steps to abolish the vestiges of aristocracy.[49] His stand vindicated the policy of the Socialist Party which had proposed that each farmer be given 12 acres of land, so that life in the rural areas could prosper. In his opinion the farmers having formed the bulk of country's population deserved better treatment. They had also played an admirable role in the freedom movement of the country.[50]

Dash represented the Baisinga Constituency of Mayurbhanj in 1957 General election as a candidate of the Socialist Party. His speeches and discourses, thereafter show more maturity and thoroughness. He acted as a member of the shadow cabinet with specialised knowledge on Forest, land reforms and peasant problems of rural Orissa. He was not carried away by cheap slogan like Industrialisation and mass employment. Prospects of village and Cottage Industries was quite dear to his heart. He castigated the Government by saying that the promises of the Second Five Year Plan were futile. He pleaded for exploiting Sabai grass and Sisal hemp of Mayurbhanj for new Industries at the village level. Among various other proposals and issues mooted by him the important ones were: (1) decentralisation of administration and due weightage to Anchal Sasan; (2) Preservation of private forests;[52] (3) Imposition of Agricultural Income Tax on the Landed aristocrats who possessed huge acreage of landed property;[53] (4) corruption during election of Speaker; (5) Inclusion of tyrannical rulers in the Council of Ministers formed by the Congress;[54](6) Abolition of privy purse of the former Rajas who had once supported Colonial Government and opposed the struggle for freedom.[55]

The most sensational revealation was the charges of corruption against the Congress Government of Harekrushna Mahtab which had favoured Biju Patnaik with a grant of £ 50,000 (approximately Rs. Ten Lakhs) for a research scheme of extracting petrol from coal. What was more surprising was the refund of Rupees Three lakhs by Patnaik through a cheque that was dishonoured by the Bank, since the loanee had no balance in his account. He also exposed the Government for paying Rs. Two Lakhs to a crook for setting up a Pilot Plant to produce Special Alloy and Steel.[56] Though the name of the crook is not mentioned in the proceedings, the deal exposed political patronage and nepotism at the higher level of the Government.

During discussion on the Appropriation Bill, 1958 Dash made categorical remark that the Government of Harekrushna Mahtab was one of rampant corruption. Such a Government was unfit to be trusted with public money. The taxation proposal was not justified. The Government had failed to tackle problems of flood and draught. It was unfit to be the custodian of the province as it was not only inefficient, but also a rubber stamp in the hands of some noted Industrialists.[57]

Dash gave a glimpse of his deep knowledge on Forest matters when he spoke at length on the leading issue during Question Answer hour. [58] He lambasted the Government for introducing no specific laws for Forest administration. Talking about the National Policy on Forest he quoted:

> Above all Forestry is one of the safest Investment as Forests are renewable assets and their exploitation can be hastened to meet the changing economic condition. xx
>
> The role of the Forest in the National economy both prospective and productive entitles to lay claim to an adequate share of land. The importance of tree lands in the rural economy of this region where agriculture constitutes the mainstay of the vast bulk of population can scarcely be over emphasised xx.
>
> No Forest Policy, however, well intentioned and meticulously drawn up, has slightest chance of success without the willing support and cooperation of the people. The recognition of their rights to forest produce at concession rates or free of royalty is not itself enough.

He observed that Orissa's forest land should increase by another 20% by expanding the present area of 24,000 sq.miles to atleast 30,000 sq.miles. By afforestation another 6000 sq.miles of forest should be created. A corporation should be setup to run the Forest administration on commercial line. There should be short term lease signed with Paper Mills, so that the State income would increase while renewing the lease. All trees should be numbered. Both Government and Private forests should be exploited equally. A comprehensive Act should replace the present Indian Forest Act of 1927.

Participating in discussion on the Orissa Irrigation Bill, 1957 Dash insisted that the bill be referred to the Select Committee because it had proposed new water cess. While the Government was eager to impose new tax on the farmers, they did nothing about the market for the products of the land. There was no foresight, no thinking ahead of problems and their solution, commented Dash.[59] He criticised the Industries Department as the most mismanaged one. Citing example of the Mining School, he said that the Government had failed to reimburse certain percentage of expenditure from the Government of India towards stipend of trainees.[60] On a subsequent occasion during voting on demands he repeatedly commented upon the mismanagement of both Industries and the Mining Department. He painfully observed how there was no technological survey to exploit the mineral wealth of Orissa. The Industries department was controlled by Private vested interests, encouraging corrupt practices. Nepotism was rampant in employment in the Industrial sector. The spinning Mills of the state were in grave plight. The Orissa Finance Corporation was niggardly in granting loans for development of Industries. Even small scale Industries were in very bad shape, he said. The state was loosing huge amount of royalty as Iron ore was not exploited to the optimum level.[61]

The Socialist in Dash favoured the idea of State trading in place of private trading. In his opinion that alone would guarantee proper price of produce. Price control was essential for a stable economy. He quoted Mehta Committee Report to say:

> Food no doubt forms the core of our price structure, but price of competing crops like cotton or oil seeds and of industrial products like cloth, fertilisers, iron and steel etc. are all very important from the point of view of an effective price policy for the country and have to bear a reasonable relationship to food prices.[62]

Without any fear or favour he again insisted upon land reforms in the context of the Orissa Tenants Relief (Amendment) Bill, 1959.[63] He criticised the inefficiency of the Government on the Appropriation Bill. He alleged that the Government was being controlled by B.Sivaraman, the Chief Secretary who was instrumental in introducing many corrupt practices.[64] He suggested prompt reorganisation of the Khadi Board. Khadi was losing popularity and importance. The Supervisors were appointed on the basis of nepotism. The Ministers were purchasing Khadi with high rebate, but not making payment, he alleged while analysing the causes of economic crisis.[65] In the context of Question and Answer he again harped on the mismanagement of Forests. He pointed out that in the name of scientific development, jungles were being destroyed. Since the Divisional Forest Officers were not visiting the spot, and the number of guards inadequate the forests were dwindling due to unauthorised cutting of trees.

Finally, when the Government brought forth the Orissa Land Reforms Bill, 1959 Dash welcomed the Bill, despite its delayed presentation. He believed that land reforms was the basis of social justice. Land should be given to the tiller. He suggested 33 acres as the highest land ceiling per family. This apart, the Government should take care to increase production. He did not agree to pay any compensation to the landlords whose excess land would be taken over for distribution by the Government.[66]

There was reason for sensitive members like Dash to lambast the Government for their failure to utilise the Plan allocation to the extent of Rs.1.5 Crore in the First Five Year Plan and Rs. 8.5 crores in the Second Five Year Plan. Since the allocation in the Third Five Year Plan was Rs. 160 crores, Dash was highly sceptic if the inept Government would be able to utilise the amount in full.[67] Similar criticism was repeated on 17 February 1961.[68]

The Government was passing through a period of instability caused by political harakiri known as horse trading. Mahtab had not been able to command majority support due to his party's unsatisfactory performance in 1957 election. The Ccngress had got only 56 seats by polling only 38% of the total votes cast. Not only there was internecine conflict in the Congress Party, but also emergence of some young and ambitious persons to grasp power. The Praja Socialist Party having won eleven seats was in a great advantage to influence the formation of Government. As the main opposition Party, the Ganatantra Parishad had 51 members under the leadership of Rajendra Narayan Singh Deo, former Raja of Bolangir and a shrewd politician. Mahtab formed the Government by encouraging defection and with the support of the nine Communist members. The tenure of Mahtab was one of the murkiest in Orissa's political history as it witnessed rampant political corruption. Mahtab had to resort to the policy of appeasement to remain in power. He patronised political corruption by showing undue favour to some mine owners and industrialists which created not only public sensation but also scandal. During the ensuing election to Rajya Sabha held in March 1958 Party discipline was thrown to the winds as Congress members resorted to cross voting. The shameless art of defection for money and power became a daily affair among the members of the Legislative Assembly. There were cases of kidnapping, illegal detention of members and physical violence. Under such unenviable situation Mahtab tendered his resignation in May 1958. But since the Congress High Command was not in favour of either imposing President's rule or opting for midterm poll, Mahtab withdrew the resignation and explored the possibility of forming a Coalition Government with the support of the Ganatantra Parishad.[69] The Coalition Government was formed on 22 May 1959. It was a marriage of convenience not destined to last long. Disappointed and disgruntled elements whose political ambition to became Ministers could not be fulfilled, decided to sabotage the coalition. Biju Patnaik a trusted lieutenant of Mahtab though initially worked as the architect of the coalition later on turned hostile. He exercised influence on the Congress High Command to remove Mahtab from power. He was young, adventurous and dynamic. His vision of a new industrialised Orissa created hopes and expectations among the young, educated unemployed voters of Orissa. His charismatic leadership made him a prospective Congress leader of the State at the cost of Mahtab. In February 1961 Biju Patnaik assumed the Presidentship of the State Congress. His first work was to dissolve the Congress-Ganatantra Parishad coalition on 24 February and the imposition of President's rule. The Mid-term Poll was scheduled for June 1961. Biju Patnaik's political star was in the ascendance as he won the election with a clear majority for the Congress Party. The Congress won 82 seats and the Praja Socialist Party got 10 seats. As a reward, Biju Patnaik adorned the chair of Chief Minister relegating Mahtab to political oblivion.[70]

Orissa witnessed three successive Congress Chief Ministers during 1961 to 1967; Biju Patnaik, Biren Mitra and Sadasiv Tripathy. The growing influence of Biju Patnaik made the Government a mere tool in serving his insatiable ambition. Power was misused. Corruption became rampant. Life in Orissa became nasty, brutish and short. Mahtab with his uncanny intelligence and R.N. Singhdeo with his complete sway over Western Orissa, started the 'oust Congress' move. Mahtab's newly formed Jana Congress Party and Singhdeo's Swatantra Party forged an electoral alliance. The Praja Socialist Party also joined with them. Sadasiv Tripathy's poor leadership and inefficient Government had to pay a heavy price. A farmers' agitation swept over Cuttack, Ganjam and Sambalpur refusing to pay water tax. Charges of corruption and administrative irregularities created sensational scandal against the Congress Party and Government. The Twenty-one Point joint election manifesto of the Opposition Parties promised ruthless elimination of corruption, and nepotism, an efficient and clean administration and setting up of

Commissions of Enquiry to investigate the charges of corruption against ministers.

The result of the 1967 election was a foregone conclusion. While the Congress won only 31 seats, the Swatantra-Jana Congress alliance won 49 and 26 seats respectively. Many Socialist leaders had campaigned in favour of the Swatantra-Jana Congress Coalition to wipe out the Congress Party from its traditional stronghold.[71] The Praja Socialist Party won 21 seats, an all time high.[72] A veteran Socialist leader like Surendra Nath Dwibedy would call it the 'Finest Hour' for the grand success of the Praja Socialist Party. The Jana Congress Party of Mahtab formed on 5 May 1966 emerged as a centre of power. It had many experienced politicians like Mahtab, Banamali Patnaik and Pabitra Mohan Pradhan etc. who favoured the idea of a coalition Government with the help of the Swatantra Party.[73] The election verdict was clearly in favour of a Coalition Government.[74] As the Praja Socialist Party was having Leftist tendencies, it could not be a part of the Coalition. They had no ideological affinity either with the Swatantra or the Jana Congress Party.

However, the Swatantra-Jana Congress having arrived at a 21-Point Common Programme before the election had to pursue a common goal as Coalition partners. They made one more addition to the Common Programme by including abolition of land revenue, the appointment of Lokayukts and Lokpals in line with the recommendations made by the Administrative Reforms Commission appointed by the Government of India and the appointment of an Inquiry Commission to probe into the corruption of Ministers who enjoyed office during June 1961 and March 1967.[75] Consequently, the Coalition Government of 1967 gave birth to several Commission of Inquiry to probe into corruption charges against Ministers. One such Inquiry Commission was the appointment of Khanna Commission as per the Home Department Notification dated 26 October 1967. Justice H.R. Khanna of Delhi High Court was entrusted to probe into seventy charges of corruption against 15 Congress Ministers/ Deputy Ministers. The list included all the three former Congress Chief Ministers, viz., Biju Patnaik, Biren Mitra and Sadasiv Tripathy who had enjoyed office during 1961 to 1967. Another Commission of Inquiry appointed by the Coalition Ministry of R.N. Singhdeo was entrusted to Mr. Justice Mudholkar, a retired Justice of the Supreme Court of India to probe into charges made against Harekrushna Mahtab.[76]

Thus, a new phase of instituting Inquiry Commission to wreck political vendetta by arch rivals in Orissa politics began from 1967 resulting in much acrimony and mud slinging which did not earn a good name to political personalities. In the floor of the Assembly, in the pages of the newspapers many sensational revelations appeared for public consumption showing clear proof of abuse of power and office. The facts proved the maxim 'Power Corrupts and absolute power corrupts absolutely'.[77]

Against the deteriorating political ethics and public morality the erstwhile leaders of the Congress Party and freedom fighters appeared to have gone astray from the ideal path of Mahatma Gandhi. But few politicians who still adhered to the Gandhian path of austerity and honesty were singled out in public assessment. They mostly belonged to the Praja Socialist Party. Although the monthly pay of a member of the Legislative Assembly was then only Rs.150/- with Dearness Allowance of Rs. 10/- per diem, the members of the Praja Socialist Group received Rs. 40 each and the rest was spent on organisational work.[78] For his personal conduct and austere life Prasanna Kumar Dash was continuously being elected by his constituencies (Baisinga and Khunta etc). He never hesitated to criticise the adventurous character and bragging nature of Biju Patnaik. In the Assembly debate both used to lock horns on matters of principles and achievements.[79] He levelled several charges of corruption against both Biju Patnaik and Biren Mitra.[80] Several cases of administrative impropriety and nepotism were brought to the notice of the public. By his fearless and unsparing criticism he could earn the unstinted support and admiration of the House. His statements were heard with rapt attention, absorbing interest and deep concern.

With growing popularity as an honest and dedicated Legislator, Dash got elected in the General elections of 1967 and 1971. The election of 1971 was a rude shock to the Socialists because the 'Garibi hatao', 'Nationalisation of Banks' and 'Abolition of the Privy purse' of former Rajas and princes gave a tremendous boost to the image of the Indian National Congress. The victory of Indian Army in the liberation of Bangladesh was another factor which contributed to the grand success of the Congress Party under the leadership of Indira Gandhi. Since Indira Gandhi could create a new image for the Congress Party, the General election of 1971 gave her a landslide victory. In Orissa the Praja Socialist Party could capture only four seats including one of Prasanna Kumar Dash in Baisinga constituency. After this victory the Congress Party came to be popularly accepted as progressive and Socialism-oriented organisation. It made the Praja Socialist Party quite redundant in the political situation of the country. An invitation was offered for the old Congress members to return to the fold of All India National Congress. This was aimed at the Praja Socialists too since they were once upon a time members of the Congress Party.[81] Other Praja Socialist leaders like Banka Behari Das, Nishamani Khuntia alongwith Prasanna Kumar Dash agreed to join the National Congress bringing an end to the Socialist forum in Orissa.

Dash admits that the above merger was not a very pleasant experience for the veteran Socialist leaders. He was almost sure that his political career would end up as an opposition member in the State Legislature. But lest people would misconstrue his joining with the Congress as a recourse to gain power or position, he was feeling very much embarrassed. He had spent almost twenty two years in the Socialist Party serving as a pivot of the Opposition in the Orissa State Assembly, and had been elected five times with an anti-Congress political stance. His only asset was his honesty and integrity. He had served his constituency with a rare commitment and zeal. However, his steadfast devotion to the cause of Socialism was a strong factor in taking the above decision to join the Congress organisation in 1971. He had firm conviction in the ideals of economic and democratic socialism. The step which he took proved to be a new turning point in his political career. There was a reorganisation of the constituencies in Mayurbhanj in 1973 leading to the abolition of Baisinga as a General constituency. Baripada was declared as the only General constituency in Mayurbhanj with nine other Reserved constituencies. This forced Dash to seek election from Baripada where he had no earlier groundwork or contact with grassroots. Consequently, for the first time in his career he lost the election by a narrow margin.[82] This was followed by many other reverses which caused great upset in his life. He lost the election to the position of President of the Mayurbhanj Urban Co-operative Bank due to the machinations of some trusted friends who turned disloyal.[83] But in the election of 1977 he got elected from Baripada constituency despite the anti-Congress wave in India which brought the Janata Government to power in Delhi and Bhubaneswar. He was elected as the Deputy leader of the

Congress Legislature Party. In the new role how he launched scathing criticism of the failures of Governments headed by Mahtab, Biju Patnaik, and others who were stalwarts in the Janata Government of 1977 created unprecedented sensation.

Against the above political scenario in Orissa and India, the performance of Prasanna Kumar Dash in the debates and proceedings of the Orissa Legislative Assembly from 1961 onwards need proper evaluation.

References

1. P.K. Dash, *Autobiography* (Oriya), p. 45. The Printing Press of Mayurbhanj was handed over.
2. H.K. Mahtab, *Autobiography* (Oriya).
3. P.K. Dash, *op. cit.*, p. 45, pp. 48-51.
4. *Ibid.*, p. 49.
5. Quoted by S.N. Dwibedy in *Quest for Socialism,* New Delhi, 1984, p. 134.
6. *Ibid.*, pp. 134-35.
7. *Ibid.*, p. 136.
8. *Ibid.*, pp. 138.
9. *Ibid.* Quoted, p. 139.
10. *Ibid.* Quoted, p. 141.
11. *Ibid.* Quoted, pp. 146-47.
12. P.K. Dash, *Op. Cit.,* pp. 48-49.
13. S. Nanda, *Coalitional Politics*, New Delhi, 1979, p. 94 and 114.
14. *Proceedings of the Orissa Legislative Assembly* (*POLA*), Vol. I, Pt. 1. No. 7, p. 17.
15. *Ibid.*, Vol. 1, Pt. 1, No. 5, pp. 37-38.
16. *Loc. cit.*
17. *Ibid.*, Vol. I, Pt. 1, No. 8, p. 27.

18. *Ibid.*, No. 10, pp. 46-47.
19. *Loc. cit.*
20. *Ibid.* No. 16, pp. 52-53.
21. *Ibid.*, No. 26, pp. 36-37.
22. *Ibid.*, Pt. 2, No. 40, pp. 35-45.
23. *Ibid.*, Vol. II, No. 6, pp. 43-44.
24. *Ibid.*, No. II, p. 32.
25. *Ibid.*, No. 14, pp. 37-38.
26. *Ibid.*, Vol. III, No. 2, p. 27.
27. *Ibid.*, No. 7, pp. 36-37.
28. *Ibid.*, No. 4, p. 30.
29. *Ibid.*, No. 22, pp. 25-30.
30. *Ibid.*, No. 28, pp. 20-22.
31. *Ibid.*, No. 29, pp. 45-47.
32. *Ibid.*, Vol. III, No. 37, p. 52ff.
33. *Ibid.*, Vol. V. No. 3, pp. 27-28.
34. *Ibid.*, No. II, pp. 36-39.
35. *Ibid.*, No. 18, pp. 21-27.
36. *Ibid.*, Vol. V, No. 26, pp. 53-56.
37. *Ibid.*, No. 33, pp. 29-30.
38. *Ibid.*, Vol. VI, No. 3, pp. 35-36.
39. *Ibid.*, No. 6, pp. 40-42.
40. *Ibid.*, No. 14, pp. 55-56.
41. *Ibid.*, No. 28, pp. 22-23.
42. *Ibid.*, No. 27, pp. 26-27.
43. *Ibid.*, No. 30, pp. 47-48.
44. *Ibid.*, Vol. III, No. 34, pp. 56-58.
45. *Ibid.*, Pt-2, No. 61.
46. *Ibid.*, Vol. VIII, No. 12, pp. 24-28.
47. *Ibid.*, No. 31, pp. 47-55.

48. *Ibid.*, Vol. VIII, No. 31, pp. 30-31.
49. *Ibid.*, Vol. VIII, Pt. 2, No. 42, pp. 40-41.
50. *Ibid.*, Vol. VIII, Pt. 2, No. 50, pp. 23-25.
51. *Ibid.*, Vol. I, Pt. 2, No. 44, pp. 16-17.
52. *Ibid.*, No. 38, p. 21.
53. *Ibid.*, p. 36.
54. *Ibid.*, p. 54.
55. *Ibid.*, p. 54.
56. *Ibid.*, pp. 27-28.
57. *Ibid.*, Vol. II, Pt. 2, No. 34, pp. 17-18.
58. *Ibid.*, Vol. III, Pt. 2, No. 2, pp. 4-5.
59. *Ibid.*, Vol. III, p. 2, pp. 28-29.
60. *Ibid.*, No. 26, pp. 29-30.
61. *Ibid.*, p. 2, No. 15, pp. 3-9 dt. 10.3.1959.
62. *Ibid.*, Vol. IV, Pt. 2, No. 13, p. 14.
63. *Ibid.*, Vol. IV, Pt. 2, No. 27, p. 18.
64. *Ibid.*, No. 26.
65. *Ibid.*, No. 34, 27 August, 1959.
66. *Ibid.*, No. 52, pp. 43-44 dt. 24.9.1959.
67. *Ibid.*, Vol. VI, Pt. 2, No. 12, dt. 11.11.1960.
68. *Ibid.*, p. 43.
69. N.K. Sahu *et al, History of Orissa,* 1`985, pp. 425-26 and S.N. Dwibedy, *op. cit.*, pp. 232-35.
70. S.N. Dwibedy, *op. cit.,* pp. 238-40.
71. N.K. Sahu etal, *op. cit.,* pp. 430-34.
72. For a comparison of figures during 1952 and 1957 elections see the Table in S.N. Dwibedy's *Quest for Socialism, op. cit.,* p. 242.
73. S. Nanda, *op. cit.,* p. 69.
74. For Party position, see S. Nanda, *op. cit.,* p. 71.
75. *Ibid.*, p. 75.

76. *Ibid.*, p. 76.
77. S.N. Dwibedy, *op. cit.,* p. 286ff.
78. P.K. Dash, *Autobiography* (Oriya), p. 58.
79. *Ibid.*, pp. 75-76.
80. *Ibid.*, pp. 77-80.
81. *Ibid.*, pp. 89-91.
82. *Ibid.*, p. 95.
83. *Ibid.*, p. 99.

3

Drummer to Speaker

National Scenario

During the Prime ministership of Indira Gandhi the Congress Party was fully under her control. Due to her authoritarian ways of handling matters and situations, many veteran Congress leaders were either marginalised or left the party to fend for themselves. Members of the Parliament, and Chief Ministers were foisted by her on the basis of their loyalty and submissive attitude. In Orissa, Harekrushna Mahtab left the Congress Party to form a new regional party of his own called the 'Jana Congress' in May 1966 with Pabitra Mohan Pradhan as the President.[1] The trend to oust Congress from power continued unabated till 1971. There was a marriage of convenience between the Swatantra and Jana Congress Parties.[2] Both the parties forged an alliance to mobilise public opinion against the Congress Government on charges of rampant corruption and inefficiency. In the election of 1967 the Congress Party in Orissa had to fight against heavy odds. With internal dissension, poor leadership and pathetic performance it could not confront against the combined attack of the Swatantra, Jana Congress and Praja Socialist Party.[3] A Kissan movement was launched against the Government with *Satyagraha*, mass demonstration, No-tax Campaign and Jail-bharo agitation. There was a Poll alliance between the Jana Congress and Swatantra Parties on the eve of the 1967 election. They drafted a Twenty-one Point Joint Programme and made suitable electoral adjustments by setting up good candidates against the Congress nominees. Their election manifesto heldout promises of honest and corruption-free administration with assurances to deliver the goods.[4]

The results of 1967 election went in favour of Swatantra-Jana Congress Coalition as they won 49 and 26 seats respectively forming a majority in the 140 member Legislature.[5] The Congress won only 31 seats. This dismal failure was a rude shock to the Congress organisation led by Biju Patnaik and the Legislative wing led by Sadasiba Tripathy. A Coalition Government was formed with R.N. Singdeo as the Chief Minister and Pabitra Mohan Pradhan as his Deputy. This Government enjoyed a smooth existence till January 1971 achieving distinction for stability and efficiency. In order to establish a clean administration the Coalition Government ceased to interfere in administration and resorted to utmost caution in financial matters. It abruptly cancelled the programme of industrial undertakings and public corporations of the previous Government. The Coalition Government had no achievement to its credit with regard to the development of the State.[6]

The stagnation created by the Swatantra-Jana Congress Coalition in the economic front facilitated the re-emergence of Biju Patnaik in Orissa politics. Since the Khanna-Commission of Inquiry exonerated Patnaik of the charges of administrative impropriety, a regrouping of political forces became inevitable. On the other hand, the charges of corruption against Harekrushna Mahtab were greatly substantiated by the Mudholkar Commission of Inquiry causing an indictment of the coalition partner. The coalition faced crisis from the Congress side whose leaders launched a protest movement.[7]

Even Mahtab's misunderstanding with Singhdeo was a cause for concern. Mahtab apprehended that Singhdeo would destroy all his political prospects by continuing further the process of Inquiry against him. As a disillusioned politician he now wanted to break the Coalition Government. But the members of the Jana Congress Party including their leader Pabitra Mohan Pradhan, the Deputy Chief Minister did not like the idea. Mahtab's threat of resignation from the party failed to have any impact.[8] The Party rejected Mahtab's idea to seek fresh mandate through a general election. Under the circumstance Mahtab toyed with the idea of joining the Congress (R) Party in order to create new image for the regional Jana Congress Party. At this juncture an unfortunate development took place in the Congress Party's selection of a candidate for the Rajya Sabha. The Congress High Command imposed Narayan Patra, a relatively unknown figure, over the choice of Biju Patnaik by the Provincial Congress Committee.[9] Patra was elected and that forced Biju Patnaik to create the Utkal Congress Party in April 1970. A chaotic situation emerged when 23 out of 31 Congress MLAs elected in 1967 to the Orissa Legislature formed the Utkal Congress Party and remaining 8 remained with the Congress (R) under Binayak Acharya as their leader in Orissa. The Opposition Party in Orissa Legislature consisted of a strange group of MLAs belonging to the Congress (O), Congress (R), Utkal Congress, Praja Socialist Party, CPI and the Jharkhand. Not only the opposition was bitterly divided and hostile in ideology, the Government of the Swatantra-Jana Congress also lacked cohesion and unity. The Jana Congress MLAs were divided in their loyalty to Mahtab and Pabitra Mohan Pradhan.[10]

The Congress (R) party under the leadership of Binayak Acharya was in a miserable state. Not only Acharya lacked both dynamism and charisma, but also Biju Patnaik's Utkal Congress Party appeared more prospective. Mahtab's position as a leader of the Jana Congress Party having been jeopardised by his own miscalculation, his change over to Congress (R) party seemed inevitable. His honeymoon with the Coalition Government was over. He negotiated with the Congress (R) leaders like Nandini Satpathy and Jagjivan Ram for defection. His image as a leader of long standing had been soiled by the Mudholkar Report. He made clandestine effort to remove Pabitra Mohan Pradhan from the leadership of Jana Congress Party by setting Surendranath Patnaik as a contender. It was expected that the rivalry between Pradhan and Patnaik would intensify intraparty conflict leading to a constitutional crisis. But Patnaik continued to support Pradhan as the leader of Jana Congress Party and the machinations of Mahtab failed.[11]

But the Coalition Government entered into rough weather on another front caused by the decision of the Swatantra Minister Hara Prasad Mohapatra to grant relaxation to Kendu leaf agents without having obtained prior Cabinet approval. As the Minister of Forest Department, Mahapatra's decision had caused a loss of revenue to the state exchequer. It provided an excuse to the Jana Congress leaders to withdraw from the Coalition Government. Mahtab highlighted the issue to criticise the Swatantra Party of corruption and 'shady deal' precisely because he wanted to precipitate a crisis.[12]

At the national level the political situation during 1969 to 1971 was boiling to a culminating point. Indira Gandhi, the Prime Minister was trying to project the Socialist image of her Congress (R) party through nationalisation of Banks and abolition of the Privy purse of the former Princes. Her popularity graph was rising very fast. But as the Supreme Court gave an adverse decision against the abolition of Privy purse and the measure failed to get the approval of the Parliament by a very narrow margin, she recommended the dissolution of the Lok Sabha in December 1970. The date fixed for midterm election to the Lok Sabha was March 1971.

The national events cast their shadow on Orissa politics where Mahtab and his followers in the Jana Congress were eager to break the Swatantra-Jana Congress Coalition. They found the Kenduleaf issue a convenient excuse to stigmatise the Swatantra Party of corrupt administrative dealings. Reluctantly Pabitra Mohan Pradhan had to join the bandwagon by handing over his resignation from the Government. He too joined the Mahtabites alleging corruption by Swatantra Ministers. Though the Chief Minister R.N. Singhdeo tried to prevent a constitutional breakdown by appointing a Cabinet Sub Committee to investigate into the controversial Kenduleaf deal of the Minister of Forest Department and stayed the implementation of the order, the Government fell. The resignation of the Jana Congress Ministers had reduced the Government of Singhdeo to a minority. Singhdeo's attempt to setup another Coalition Government with the support of Utkal Congress Party did not materialise. Ultimately, he resigned on 9 January 1971 and president's rule was imposed in Orissa. But before tendering resignation, he had appointed (on 6 January 1971) a Commission of Inquiry by Justice Sarjoo Prasad to probe into the corruption charges against Mahtab as suggested by Justice Mudholkar. The deepening crisis precipitated the course for holding a midterm election in 1971 in Orisssa alongwith the Lok Sabha polls.

Mahtab showed no compunction to join the Congress (R) party on 15 January 1971 and was followed by several others.[14] He did not spare any pain to regain his hold on Orissa politics by swelling his follower's strength. For him it was a question of survival while saving the image that he had created as a veteran politician. But in his quest for survival he created political instability that precipitated the imposition of President's rule from 11 January to 3 April 1971 and the mid term election which further accentuated horse trading with all the resultant evils.[15]

After the elections in March 1971 the political picture in Orissa continued to be as confused as in 1967 since none of the contending parties could attain absolute majority in the Legislative Assembly. The results showed the Utkal Congress with 33, the Swatantra Party with 36, the Jharkhand with 4, the Jana Congress with 1, Congress (O) with 1, Congress (R) with 49, Communists with 6, Socialists with 4 and Independent with 1 members.[16] On 3 April 1971 the United Front coalition comprising of the Utkal Congress, Swatantra and Jharkhand Parties under the leadership of Biswanath Das formed the popular Government which could not survive long in an atmosphere of unscrupulous political behaviour.[17] While the Utkal Congress as a whole decided to merge with the Congress (R) there were large scale defections from the Swatantra and Jharkhand Parties. Four Praja Socialist MLAs also joined with the Congress (R). The Congress (R) party now having a strength of 94 members on 10 June 1972 elected Nandini Satpathy as the Leader of the Congress Legislature Party and took the oath of office as Chief Minister on 14 June.[18]

Although Satpathy had the support of a clear majority, the life her Government was far from safety. The refusal of the Congress (R) High Command to admit top six leaders of the Utkal Congress Party including Biju Patnaik, created a very unfortunate situation which marked the beginning of troubles. Patnaik withdrew the erstwhile members of the Utkal

Congress from Satpathy's Government and formed the Pragati Dal with Swatantra and some followers of Mahtab. The formation of the Pragati Dal sounded the death knell of Satapathy's Government. Satpathy resigned on 1 March 1973 while recommending the dissolution of the Assembly.[19] Though Biju Patnaik, the leader of the Pragati Dal claimed the support of 72 members of the Assembly, the Governor did not offer him a chance to form the Government. Not that the Governor was unaware of the majority support behind Patnaik's claim, but he expressed doubts about the stability of the proposed Government and recommended the dissolution of the Assembly to the President. His arguments were : (*i*) Satpathy had not lost her majority support while tendering resignation; (*ii*) political defections in the State had formed a regular feature jeopardising smooth functioning of democracy; (*iii*) the Legislators had no moral scruples to change their parties for gaining office of profit; and (*iv*) the Pragati Dal was ideologically not a cohesive organisation.[20]

The Assembly was dissolved and Orissa again came under the President's rule with effect from 3 March 1973. According to political analysts the action of the Governor was not as per the provisions of the constitution. His action was motivated and smacked of partisan spirit. He not only tried to save the Congress Government of Satpathy from defeat in the Legislature, but also denied the opposition of an opportunity to form the Government. Biju Patnaik ought to have been invited to form the Government on the day Satpathy tendered her resignation as the Chief Minister. So the Governor's recommendation for the dissolution of the Legislative Assembly was unfair. The Honourable Orissa High Court held that the Governor did not follow the correct Parliamentary conventions.[21]

Thus, Orissa had to face another mid term election in February 1974. The election failed to give absolute majority to any political party. Yet Nandini Satpathy claimed the privilege to form Government with the support of the CPI members in the new Assembly. On 6 March 1974 she took the oath of office along with 16 members of the ministry. The Governor was vehemently criticised by the Pragati Dal and others for having allowed a minority party like the Congress (R) to form the Government.[22]

Satpathy's second tenure as the Chief Minister of Orissa, notwithstanding the support of 69 Congress MLAs was seriously handicapped by internal dissension in the Party. The first sound of revolt against her leadership was raised by prominent ministers like Banka Behary Das who was originally a Socialist member. After his resignation Binayak Acharya, the second man in the Cabinet raised the standard of revolt. Acharya demanded a change in the Party leadership on ground that Satpathy patronised Yuva Chhatra Sangram Samiti and the Nationalist Corps under her son Tathagata's leadership as a parallel organisation of the Youth Congress. There were other serious charges of corruption and misuse of administrative powers during the Emergency period.[23] Out of 69 Congress MLAs as many as 42 demanded a change of leadership. Under the advice of the Prime Minister, Satpathy resigned on 16 December 1976. The Governor suspended the Assembly and proclaimed President's rule which lasted up to 29 December when Binayak Acharya was sworn in as the Chief Minister.[24]

However, the Congress Party's record of performance during the Chief Ministership of Satpathy and Acharya was far from satisfactory. Apart from the excesses committed during emergency in the form of censorship of the Press and large scale imprisonment of political leaders, the defection in the party and intra-party feuds had seriously damaged the Congress organisation. Therefore, the prospect of winning an election with decisive majority votes was quite bleak. A non-Congress ministry was formed at the National level after the March 1977 election to the Lok Sabha.[25] Following this unexpected change at the Centre, the Congress Governments in nine States including Orissa were dismissed by the President under Article 356. The requirement of seeking a report from the Governor was not resorted to. Since the Governors had been appointed by the Congress Prime Minister there was a suspicion that the Governors would not recommend the dissolution of the Legislature. The dissolution of nine State Assemblies created great hue and cry in the political circle. In Orissa the Congress Party under the leadership of Binayak Acharya prepared to face the electorate with a lack lustre record in office. The State came under the rule of the President for a short spell from 30 April 1977 to 26 June.[26]

The midterm election of June 1977 witnessed great euphoria against the Congress party which was responsible and condemned vigorously for the Emergency. On 25 June 1975, the President of India had proclaimed a State of Emergency in exercise of the powers conferred on him by Article 352 (Clause I) of the Constitution. The proclamation stated that a grave emergency exists whereby the security of India is threatened by internal disturbance. Three factors had forced Smt Indira Gandhi to impose her Emergency rule. These were:

(1) The opposition was out to paralyse the Government, undermine the democratic Institutions and disrupt the economy of the country.

(2) Certain persons had started inciting the armed forces to mutiny and the Police force to rebel. Anti-Congress parties had drawn a programme of Civil disobedience and to obstruct

normal functioning of the Government and economy.

(3) The forces of disintegration were at full play and communal passions were being aroused threatening the discipline of the nation and stability of the Government.

Confirming the Presidential proclamation, the Parliament resolved, "The term justification for the present proclamation of Emergency under Article 352 of the constitution is the preservation of public good".[28] The Emergency was the logical culmination of Smt. Gandhi's style of functioning and temperament. She was a champion of authoritarian populism.

During the short period of Emergency there was the gradual erosion of Rule of Law and marginalisation of the provisions of the constitution. She followed the dictum one leader, one Party, no dissent within the Party. The authority of the Judiciary was drastically curtailed. MISA (Maintenance of Internal Security Act) was amended to keep the judiciary from reviewing the reasons of detention. Democratic rights of the citizens and strike by workers were severely restrained. The political system was centralised.

Prasanna Kumar Dash was nominated as the Congress candidate for Baripada constituency. The veteran leader agreed to campaign from Baripada alone, undeterred by the anti-Congress emotion which was running high among the electorates. Since he was not associated with power in the Emergency period he had no problem or fear to face the voter's ire. Chaitanya Prasad Majhi, the Congress candidate from Mayurbhanj had lost the Lok Sabha election a short while ago. The serious jolt received by the Congress Party at the Parliamentary election was quite fresh in the memory. So the contest between Prasanna Kumar Dash as Congress candidate and his rival P.C. Bhanjdeo of the former ruling family evoked great interest among the public. The contest was triangular one involving the Congress, the Jana Congress and the

Independent candidates. Disproving the worst fear of all, Prasanna Kumar Dash got elected for the sixth time defeating his nearest rival by a margin of 2200 votes. Since he was the only General candidate from Mayurbhanj, the voters expected him to represent the interests of the district vigorously and truthfully.

In the above election only 27 Congress candidates had been elected to the Orissa Legislative Assembly. The Congress members elected Chintamani Panigrahi and Prasanna Kumar Dash as their leader and Deputy leader respectively in the Legislature. A profound change in the Orissa politics was evident due to the formation of a non-Congress Government after almost thirty years. Though it was the Government of the Janata Party, the leaders were once upon a time stalwarts of the Congress Party. Nilamani Routroy, the Chief Minister, Biju Patnaik, the Janata Minister of Steel and Mines at the centre and Dr. H.K. Mahtab, the Pro-Janata leader, were all in the Congress party a few years ago. They had enjoyed considerable clout in Orissa Politics since the Independence. After being saddled in power, they had adopted a strong anti-Congress stance. For the Congress Party to sit in the opposition was quite a new experience. But it was not different with Prasanna Kumar Dash. Althrough his induction to the Legislative Assembly as a member, he had been thoroughly baptised in the art of critically analysing the Government policies and ineptitude. He had never been inducted to the Council of Ministers despite his vast experience as a Legislator and thorough knowledge about the problems facing the State. He analysed how long the Janata leaders were either running the Government or associated with it and their contributions to Orissa's miserable state of economy and backwardness. As Deputy leader of the Congress Legislature Party he compared the Janata leaders with Legendary Ratnakara who turned Balmiki and held them squarely accountable for the gross mismanagement of the administrative affairs in Orissa.[29] The satirical criticism was found to be very effective.

In the newly elected Assembly, while taking part in proposing a vote of thanks on the Governor's address, Dash observed that the speech was meaningless since there was no indication of the Government's future vision of Orissa. Nothing had been said on Agriculture, Industries or economic policies. He urged upon the Government to have a definite Industrial policy for the future generation. He criticised the rising price index of essential commodities and demanded progressive land reforms. He pleaded for decentralisation of administrative powers and responsibilities. While controlling the bureaucrats for a welfare oriented Government. He expressed his firm belief on democratic values and democratic tradition in India. At the same time he expected the integration of the country to be kept in mind.[30]

Nothing provoked the analytical mind of Dash more than a discussion on the annual budget of the State. He was very unhappy over the Government's lack of direction and proper outlook. He lamented over the lethargy of the Government in bringing down prices of consumers goods, failure to tackle the problems of unemployment, enforcing prohibition and solving the difficulties of the rural population.[31] He felt highly agitated over the inefficiency in Police administration and rampant corruption therein. The top heavy administration of the Police department was a drain on public exchequer, he said.[32] Drawing the Chief Minister's attention to promote agriculture, he said that Irrigation and Power should be given equal weightage. Emphasis should also be given to Irrigation through Rural electrification to increase agricultural production.[33] In course of a debate on the budget of the Supply Department, he advised the concerned Ministry to check price rise of edible oil, clothes and rice.[34] Considering Indian public attitude for indigenous medicine he suggested the Government to open Ayurvedic and homeopathic dispensaries in the Rural areas. To prevent exploitation by unscrupulous Quacks he advised the Health Department to ensure the registration of medical practitioners in the villages.[35]

Opening the debate on the Reappropriation Bill, Dash got an opportunity to analyse the nature and impact of administration run by the Janata Party. He observed that 85% people in Orissa were below the poverty line. The Government was stagnant and ineffective. Many were resorting to strike and agitation. Crime like robbery was increasing. Employment of the Oriyas was being ignored by the authorities in Rourkela Steel Plant. He alleged that the Chief Minister was a victim of Non-Oriya clique.[36] When the Gram Panchayat Bill was put to vote Dash preferred to discuss its provisions threadbare. He took pains to throw light on the disciplinary procedure to ensure a corruption free administration based on transparency and accountability.[37] As the Government proposed an Agricultural Income Tax Bill, Dash in order to save the farmers from unnecessary harassment cautioned the Government agency to be very careful in making assessment.[38] An amendment tc the Universities Act was tabled by the Government with a view to give representation to the Students in the Senate. Dash supported the amendment as a progressive step. While talking on the policy of prohibition he observed that the Government was not sincere in enforcing prohibition for the fear of loosing revenue.

Dash was very much concerned at the prevailing regional imbalance in Orissa which he wanted to be eradicated. He observed that many senior posts in the Food Corporation of India and the Rourkela Steel Plant were lost on account of the callousness of the Government.[39] He did not like misuse of power by the bureaucrats and Ministers. He proposed a cut motion on the

(*i*) Misuse of Staff Cars by Ministers;

(*ii*) Increasing expenses in the Secretariat;

(*iii*) Slow disposal of files

(*iv*) For better expertise Technical persons to be appointed as Additional Secretaries in Departments such as Agriculture, Industries, works and Health Services etc.

He was in favour of interchange of Staff between the Secretariat and the Heads of Departments. To prevent corruption, he wanted the Vigilance Department to be more effective. He vehemently criticised the Chief Minister for his undue interest in the Home Department affairs. During the vote on account debate, he castigated the Police administration calling upon the high officials to stop misusing staff cars so as to economise the expenses. He lamented over the declining standard of Orissa Public Service Commission. The Judiciary Department also came under his unsparing criticism. A firm believer in the maxim "Justice delayed is justice denied" he observed that the Judiciary needed toning up to dispose off numerous pending cases. Quoting a white paper published by the Government, he informed the house that crimes in the State were increasing despite numerous IPS officers in the top. In comparison to Uttar Pradesh he found the cadre strength of IPS officers in Orissa was higher. But since the crime graph was ascending he failed to findout the justification in having a top heavy administration.[40]

Dash always retained his rural background and took proper care of his constituency. He felt mortified to find inefficiency, corruption and gross mismanagement in the Panchayati Raj department. He alleged how grants for

Panchayat Welfare were being misused. Funds were needed for education, agriculture and health. More grants were required for Tribal welfare, labour welfare, Deaf and Dumb Schools, Nutrition programme and prison welfare. He wished the Government to be vigilant against juvenile delinquency, Immoral traffic and grant of old age pension etc.[41]

In the context of a cut motion on the Department of Agriculture and Cooperative, Dash observed that agriculture in Orissa never showed a stable rate of production since it was not organised on scientific lines. The Government have employed more staff/personnel without ensuring proportionate increase in production. A Statistical report published by the Government on the basis of Dr. N. Rath's studies proved how Orissa was not as progressive as other Indian States. The reasons were traced to ineffective Extension Programme and poor marketing facilities. There was rampant corruption in the cooperative Societies.[42]

The Forest Department often evoked special interest of Dash. He was a born apostle of ecological balance. Protection of natural Forest was his cherished goal. Since he wanted to improve the Forest wealth of Orissa, the lack of a working plan and reluctance to invest funds appeared quite painful to him. He referred to the denudation of Simlipal Hills, the reckless administration of Kenduleaf trade and absence of a working plan for bamboo forest.[43]

The Budget session of the Assembly offered an opportunity to comment upon the state of Government. It was time for the Sixth Five Year Plan layout to be finalised. The MLAs expected the policy outline to have been incorporated in the Address of the Governor. To his utter dismay Dash saw such major lapses of the Government policy makers. Due to inefficient Government machinery, Plan expenditures had not been completed. The Government's failure in having a corruption-free-administration, in guaranteeing democratic rights to the people, in controlling price Index, in solving unemployment problem and last of all in removing regional imbalances had been quite conspicuous. The Governor in his Address said nothing on these accounts; nor did he say anything on irrigation, roads and communication and other allied aspects of public interest.[44] He discussed on Land reforms in Orissa (Amendment) as a very important issue before the Legislature. Explaining that Indian economy and culture had an agricultural base, he called upon the fellow Legislators to develop a strong political will in proper classification of land and its distribution.[45] The distribution of surplus land needed careful handling, he cautioned. A few days later he discussed the problems of Secondary education in Orissa and teachers working in the Schools.[46] Thus, he made proper use of the Legislature as a Public forum to ventilate various problems of the State besides urging upon the Government to rise to the occasion in doing good to the people.

The political barometer in the country was recording a rise in the temperature. There was growing dissension in the Congress Party over the issue of Indira Gandhi's leadership which came under fire on account of the misuse of power during Emergency. The dissension led to a division of the party as Congress (I) and Congress (S). Indira Gandhi's group was formed as Congress (I) in 1978. She fought for a Lok Sabha seat from Chikmagalur constituency in Karnatak and won the election with wide margin of votes over her nearest rival. The Janta Government at the centre too was facing internal trouble due to a triangular struggle for power. The leaders involved in the struggle were Morarjee Desai, Charan Singh and Devilal. Internal feuds in the Janata Government precipitated events towards the midterm Lok Sabha election in January 1980 (3 and 6 January 1980). Forgetting the excesses of the Emergency period, the Indian electorates gave a fresh mandate to Smt. Gandhi whose Congress (I) Party won nearly two thirds of the seats in the Lok Sabha. The victory restored her dominance in the Party and the Party's hegemony in Indian politics. The old Congress was no more as the old Guards had either retired or died. Smt. Gandhi returned to power with new vigour and new mandate. The Congress (I) organisation had been rejuvenated. As the head of the Party she most carefully centralised political power in her person to ensure her Leviathan-like grip over the political system. Notwithstanding the preponderance of one person, the change ushered in was ominous for the prospect of Parliamentary democracy in India. Party and Parliamentary democracy began to decay as all sections of the people and Institutions became politicised. It was rightly commented that,

> At no time in independent India's history, the liberal political order was in more peril than under the personalised and centralised power wielded by Mrs. Gandhi with all the paraphernalia of the mechanism of coercion at its disposal.[47]

After the dust of the General elections to the Seventh Lok Sabha settled down and Smt. Gandhi had at her command the massive support of 351 Congress (I) members, she decided to dissolve the Legislative Assemblies of nine Indian States (Uttar Pradesh, Madhya Pradesh, Bihar, Rajasthan, Punjab, Orissa, Gujarat, Maharashtra and Tamilnadu). The decision was taken on 17 February 1980 at an urgent meeting of the Cabinet. The precedence for such action was found in the events of 1977 when the Janata Government of Morarjee Desai had dissolved the Congress Governments of seven states. The proclamation issued by the President did not gkve any reason of dissolution. It merely took legal shelter under the Article 356 of the Constitution which empowers the

Centre to dismiss the Provincial Governments. The deck was cleared for midterm election in all the nine States two years before the same was due. Explaining the reason for dismissal, the Party Spokesmen said that since the Congress (I) was voted to power at the Centre, the non-Congress Governments in the States were required to have a fresh mandate from the people to rule. Similar reason had been furnished by the Janata Government in 1977 when the Congress Governments in seven states were dismissed. The decision taken in 1980 was in consonance with the above convention and compatible to Smt. Gandhi's temperament. In 1977 commenting upon the Janata Government's "Politics of dissolution" Smt. Gandhi had condemned the decision as undemocratic and fascist. But why she took identical decision in 1980 was apparently clear. She was aware that the Congress (I) was a minority in the Rajya Sabha and One third of the total members in the Rajya Sabha were to retire on 12 April 1980. She apprehended that if elections were not held in the states replacing the Janata Governments by Congress (I) Governments, she would not be in a position to change the composition of the Rajya Sabha. That would jeopardise her position in the Upper House as well as her political manoeuvrability. Thus, expediency dictated her policy decision in February 1980 to dissolve the Legislative Assemblies in as many as nine states.

In Orissa the midterm elections were scheduled to be held in May 1980. Prasanna Kumar Dash had joined the Congress (I) Party. Though there was a misgiving about his nomination for Baripada constituency, the party fielded him against Pramod Chandra Bhanj Deo, a strong contender. The District Election Committee was reluctant to recommend his name; but Party High Command on the basis of Intelligence report approved his nomination. Though Bhanjdeo was an Independent candidate, he had large support-base. But Dash won the election for a record seventh time as Member of the Legislative Assembly. Out of 146 seats, the Congress (I) won 117 seats. Remaining seat distribution showed—Lok Dal 13, Janata Party 3, Congress (S) 2, CPI 2 and Independents 7. Janaki Ballabh Patnaik who had served as the Minister of State for Defence, was elected Leader of the Congress (I) Legislature Party to form the Government. Patnaik chose Kaunria Majhi and Saraswati Hembram, two tribal MLAs from Mayurbhanj as members of the Council of Ministers. Dash was made the Chairman of Public Undertaking Committee to act as a watchdog on the Government sponsored undertakings. While visiting some of the undertakings he tried to uphold the principle of honesty by refusing free hospitality and leading a modest lifestyle befitting a true Gandhian. Power never swayed him from the ideal of simple living and noble thinking and by that standard he always tried to assess others who worked with him as his colleagues or associates. Loss of a ministerial berth never disappointed him as much as it agitated his associates. He took it sportively in his political strides. He got a few years more to serve the Legislature as a very matured member of the Assembly and thereby enriched the proceedings of the House. As a member of the Congress Legislature Party his strident criticism of the deficiencies of the Government of the Congress often caused tremor in the Party circle. But his role as a critic was appreciated by all and sundry, since it was well known as to the mould in which he was cast from the beginning of his career as a Legislator.

Beginning with the debate on Governor's address to the newly elected Assembly in 1980 till 1984 (22 February) when he was unanimously elected as the Speaker, Prasanna Kumar Dash remained true to the high ideals of Parliamentary democracy. The following discussion will illustrate the role that he played showing neither fear nor favour to any body. During the above period he created a permanent niche for himself as the Protector of Orissan ecology by promoting the study of Environment and mooted several projects for the good of humanity. That would be enlisted as his permanent contribution as a Member of the Orissa Legislative Assembly.

After Listening to the Governor's Address to the new House Dash felt happy over the assurance given to ameliorate the condition of the poor people in Orissa. The Government committed themselves to help during the next five years 5 lakhs people in the economic progress. Scheme such as granting of old age pension and the distribution of land to the landless were in the cards. He supported the Government decision to stop private practice by Doctors working in the three Medical Colleges and wanted the decision to be rigorously enforced. He urged upon the Government of Janaki Ballabh Patnaik to sanction more funds for agriculture and irrigation. The promise made by Patnaik to invest Rupees 500 Crores in five years period on Industrialisation created large scale euphoria. Dash called upon the opposition Parties to cooperate with the Government to promote cottage Industries and small scale industries. The activities of the District Industrial centres should be reviewed, he said. He had rightly observed how the noncooperation of the Orissa State Electricity Board was thwarting the programme and activities of the DICs since there could be no industry without power. In his opinion, agriculture being the main prop of state economy, the Government would better accord Priority to investment on Irrigation measures through Dug wells, Tube wells, Minor Irrigation Projects and take permanent steps to prevent flood and famine.[48]

The debate on Orissa State Electricity Board gave Dash an opportunity to trace its slow development. He wished the scheme of electrification to spread to the villages even if such expansion required availing of loans with State guarantee. The efficiency of the Board was to improve by better management and not by corrupt practices such as appointment of NMR workers. To prevent corruption he advised the Board Engineers to take list of casual workers from the local Employment Exchange.[49]

Das complained against rising price index of essential commodities while pleading before the Government to reduce inflation. In view of draught in the previous year there was less production of paddy and inadequate supply of foodgrains to Mayurbhanj, his home district. In his opinion there was scope for the Food Corporation of India to improve upon the existing system of distribution to ensure better supply to the urban areas. He brought the inefficiency of the Supply Department also under focus. He advised the department to tone-up the Public distribution system with a touch of honesty and sincerity.[50]

On a later occasion, he analysed the working of the Irrigation Department and requested the Government to place more funds. He cautioned against poor water resources management saying that both excess and scarcity of water had their baneful effect on state economy. The debate speech delivered by him showed the depth of his intensive research based knowledge about the problems facing the Department. He made comparison and quoted statistics to drive home the points under focus. The top heavy administration of the Engineering Department was giving a disappointing performance, he lamented with concern.[51] He was unhappy with the discriminatory treatment of the Government which had shown indifferent attitude towards Mayurbhanj precipitating regional imbalance. How Mayurbhanj was not treated at par with the coastal districts was apparent in the delay to expedite the Suvarnarekha Irrigation Project. Although after agreement was signed with Bihar, and Patna had posted the Chief Engineer to look after their portion of the Project, the Orissa Government had not even appointed an Executive Engineer. The move of the Government to avail World Bank loan was slow and frustrating. He recalled the contributions made by the Rajas of Mayurbhanj in establishing Ravenshaw College, Engineering and Medical Schools at Cuttack in the past and demanded reciprocity as a token of gratitude. He made stunning revelation about the cracks in the Hirakud Dam which the Government had kept a well guarded secret. Casting severe displeasure against the thoroughly corrupt Orissa State Electricity Board, he suggested for its abolition. He made his annoyance clear because the Board was not cooperating with the Lift Irrigation Department, thereby thwarting the development of agriculture. Making a Cassandra like profession, he said

> Let us try to harness the opportunity for the people of Orissa, otherwise if the future of Orissa is not promoted through Irrigation, we will go to Calcutta to work as Coolies.[52]

While supporting the Appropriation Bill, Dash drew the attention of the Chief Minister to the devastations caused by flood and the failure of the Government to control public expenditure through proper planning. Many Government departments having failed to reach the target received his displeasure, particularly the Departments of Irrigation, Power and Agriculture. Even in a crucial department like Agriculture, plan expenditure was not being monitored. No step had been taken to develop human resources. The State was facing acute shortage of technical personnel. Nothing had been done to develop cummunication. He strongly felt that the reorganisation of administrative machinery was essential. He wished to review the working of the District Industrial centres. There was need to promote private industries as that way employment could be generated. He wanted to know the utility of the IPICOL (Industrial Promotion and Infrastructure Corporation Limited). With a note of bitter sarcasm he pointed out that the Simlipal Development Corporation was merely cutting the trees whose consequences would be disastrous. Adding a note of caution he asked the Government to preserve and develop the Forest wealth in the State. He did not hesitate to point out the mismanagement of the Supply Department. How in the Sixth Plan period the educated unemployed would get more employment opportunities worried him constantly.[53]

In October a Bill to amend the Cooperative Act was tabled before the Assembly. Dash saw enough reasons to drastically amend the Act so as to make provision for the appointment of Technical Experts at the helm of affairs. He did not approve of the idea of getting Experts on deputation from other Departments.[54] The snail speed with which work was progressing in the Simlipal National Park was equally frustrating. As long as the tribals continue to live in their existing habitations, they would continue to destroy the forest. The Simlipal Development Corporation was having more officers than the actual requirement. They were busy not in development, but in exploitation. He urged upon the Government to stop the ruthless deforestation work that was going on. If Simlipal disappeared, there would be natural calamities like tornado. He scoffed at the wisdom of planting Eucalyptus in place of Sal trees. The destruction of Simlipal would spell doom upon Orissa. He made an earnest appeal to the Minister of Forests to maintain the ecological balance by preserving forest wealth.[55] There was a full fledged debate on Simlipal on 6 October 1980 which would go down in the history of Ecology in Orissa as a landmark for its vision and prophetic utterances. The way Simlipal was being devastated pained him most. He enquired if the Minister of Forest had ever visited Simlipal and expressed his deep concern for its protection. He called upon the fellow MLAs to realise the gravity of the situation and to advise the Government to seek the assistance of the UNESCO. In his concern for Simlipal he had made in-depth study of various reports and statistics. He criticised the indifferent attitude of the public and commented upon the Simlipal Project Report as incorrect. He read a portion of the said Report:

> As already stated Simlipal forests have been over exploited in the past. There has been no Input to improve the crop. The Giant Champa, Peeasal trrees are no longer to be seen. Blanks have been created in the recent cyclone and Euphoria has taken possession of the grounds. Natural regeneration of principal species will be a problem in these areas unless they are established by artificial regeneration.[56]

The debate on Simlipal continued further giving opportunity to many other members to participate and express their views. Finally, Dash moved a motion to constitute a House Committee on Simlipal. The motion read,

> That a Committee of the House be formed consisting of the following members to see the activities of the Simlipal Development Forest Corporation and undertake visits to the concerned areas of the Simlipal Hills and advise the Government in respect of proper development.

1. Speaker
2. Minister of State for Forest, Fisheries and Animal Husbandry
3. Sri Prasanna Kumar Dash, M.L.A.

4. Sri Bipin Das, Govt. Chief Whip
5. Sri Prasanna Kumar Pal, Govt. Deputy Chief Whip.
6. Sri Bhupinder Singh, MLA
7. Sri Sunder Mohan Majhi, MLA
8. Sri Sarat Kumar Deb, MLA
9. Sri Udaynarayan Deb, MLA
10. Sri Haladhar Mishra, MLA
11. Sri Biswanath Sahu, MLA
12. Sri Kangoi Singh, MLA

The motion was adopted on 9 March 1981.[57]

Taking part in the discussion for Budget demand on Irrigation and Power Department, Prasanna Kumar Dash observed that Irrigation and Power held keys to the economic progress of a country. Without these two forces economy would not show any improvement. He was bitter for the neglect shown to Rural electrification. He was aware of the miserable state of finance prevailing in the Orissa State Electricity Board. The Board had a loan burden of Rupees 365 crores. Their financial position was deteriorating for non-collection of Power tariff. All Projects were not working to capacity and the short fall in power requirement of the State continued. There was no sincerity in expediting the Suvarnarekha Project, Dash observed, saying that the Chief Engineer was yet to be posted. His expectation that the project would start operating in 1980-81 was belied.[58]

Looking backward to the regime of the Janata Government, Dash bluntly stated that nothing was done in the Power sector. He was, however, thankful to the Congress Government for having introduced schemes like the Old Age Pension as a welfare measure. People should wait for some time to get results of other welfare schemes of the new Congress Government which had been in office for last few months. But he assured the people to pursue the matters of development through government agencies, Citing examples of the Governments' commitment to ensure economic progress, he spoke about the recent foundation stone laying ceremony by Prime Minister Indira Gandhi of an Alumina Project costing Rupees 1500 crores. It was the beginning of a giant stride to promote employment opportunities. Referring to the Plan layout he insisted upon utilising the grant within the stipulated time as otherwise Projects would remain incomplete and the path of progress would be thwarted. With his inside knowledge about the bad financial management, he observed that both surplus and deficit were equally baneful and undesirable. Corruption prevailing in the departments need to be uprooted. The Ministers were asked by him to control the corrupt officials and he would not accept last moment surrender of plan allocation. In his opinion 'Efficiency' should be the watchword of bureaucracy and that would be a matter of pride for all. He reminded the Government to make a comparison with the neighbouring states while planning Agricultural and Industrial schemes. Since the Per capita Income of Orissa was Rupees 245/- against Rupees 361/- in Bengal, Rupees 329/- in Andhra Pradesh, Rupees 512/- in Haryana and Rupees 611/- in Punjab, the Government must bear in mind the difficult task ahead.[59]

Elaborating the points further, Dash observed that Orissa would require huge Technical manpower in the Sixth Plan period. Our Engineering Schools and Colleges were not adequate. He lamented over the fact that the Government of Orissa did not have any forward planning. The ITDP and TRW grants to the tune of Crores have gone in vain leaving no impact on the Tribal population. The Government had not made any plan for rural electrification and agriculture had not been given due weightage. The Department of Agriculture had more officers than the actual need. He wanted to know what was their contribution to the growth of agricultural production in the state. The consumer prices were increasing. He did not hesitate to criticise the Public undertakings as 'white elephants' and the districts of Mayurbhanj, Kalahandi, Bolangir and Phulbani being utterly neglected. He called upon the Government to treat each district as a separate unit to make proper assessment of economic growth.[60]

Dash exposed a shoddy deal on the production of charcoal involving the Chief Conservator of Forest and the IMFA (Indian Metals and Ferro-Alloys) of Bansidhar Panda, a leading Industrialist of Orissa. Both being relations their clandestine deal had caused a loss of Rupees 3 cores to the state exchequer. This was an example of administrative impropriety and misuse of power.[61] He supported the Aided Educational Institutions (Appointment of Teachers Validation) Bill. This was necessary to regularise the services of adhoc teachers/lecturers who had failed to qualify before the Orissa Public Service Commission. The Government adopted a compassionate attitude to retain the unfortunate lot in services on account of the fact that the Orissa Public Service Commission were most irregular in holding interviews/tests. Since teachers/ lecturers who had served for 5 to 8 years had been retrenched, Dash made an appeal to the Education Minister to regularise their services and to stop further appointments on adhoc basis.[62]

The Government proposed to established a Sanskrit University in Orissa to promote Sanskrit studies and brought a motion adopting the establishment of Sri Jagannath Sanskrit Viswavidyalaya at Puri. Dash was glad to support the Bill for its lofty ideal and suggested the affiliation of all Sanskrit

Schools under the above University. Puri, on account of its long tradition as a centre of Sanskrit learning and scholarship was the befitting place for location of the proposed University.[63]

The problem facing the Cooperative Societies came before the Assembly for discussion. Although Dash was aware of the contributions of the Regional Cooperative Marketing Society in facilitating economic changes in the rural areas/villages he wanted to be informed by the Government about the action taken against corrupt officials and the misuse of funds. He expected the officers to manage the godowns properly to prevent pilferage and corruption.[64]

The Assembly also discussed about the working of the Supply Department. Dash informed the House that the Government had no control over the rising prices caused by inadequate supply of essential consumer items. He blamed the millowners for their failure to balance between demand and supply. That year rice procurement was not satisfactory for which the defaulting Agents' license should be cancelled, he said. He asked the Government to let the House know why procurement was inadequate if the harvest was good. In his own calculation he had felt that the harvest was poor. He placed before the House the problem created by short supply of cement and sugar. He felt that the Government run Fair Price shops were not being managed well.[65]

The above debate was followed by discussion on Irrigation budget. Though he supported the demand for grant he grilled the Government for their failure to utilise the World Bank loan on medium and major Irrigation projects. The delay over the implementation of Suvarnarekha Project was very painful to him. He had pinned much hope on the Project for a face lift of the economy of the people of his district

Mayurbhanj. Since Irrigation was the key to economic progress, the Department should get Top priority treatment in Government Agenda. The Government's policy should aim at uplift of whole state, not any particular areas. The Governments Irrigation Policy for the Sixth Plan should be accordingly formulated. Referring back to Suvarnarekha Irrigation Project, the non-appointment of the field staff like the SDO, and Assistant Engineer etc. disappointed him. That Bihar Government had done more work and Orissa had spent only Rupees 42 crores provoked profound bitterness in his mind producing deep scepticism. The estimate for the reservoir was yet to be completed and acquisition of forest land had not been completed. With an agitated mind he threatened to lunch public agitation in case the work would not start in 1982-83. His own constituency being draught prone, Dash insisted upon the Government to create a Lift Irrigation Division there.[66]

Dash was not in favour of Budget deficit since it created situation to go for overdraft. He exposed the clever manipulation of the Bureaucracy responsible for financial management in the state. He did not hesitate to point out that the bureaucracy could make deficit budget a Surplus one by incurring no expenditure for nine months in a financial year and by keeping several checks in the process of releasing funds called letters of credit. Analysing the cause of Orissa's poverty and low rate in the per capita income, he blamed the previous leadership and was happy that the existing Government had started 14 large scale and 35 medium scale industries. This was a positive step to boost up peoples' economy. Since the Legislature was approving an annual budget of Rupees 600 crores, he rightly expected relative prosperity. He made a detailed discussion of the problems of Inflation and Spiralling of prices and their impact on Budget. Likewise, explaining the miserable condition of State Sponsored Public undertakings he preferred their closure. Expenses incurred on Draught relief and anti-Draught measures showed no result for misuse of funds and misappropriation. If the Government had spent money on Irrigation why production did not increase, was a valid question parried by him to his own Party's Government.[67]

During 'Half an hour' discussion on 16 March 1982 Dash highlighted the agonising state of Industries in Mayurbhanj. The District was having only three Industries: Baripada Spinning Mill, East Coast Fertilisers and Chemicals and NICO (National Insulated Cable Company). In these Industries the local people were denied with employment opportunities through nepotism and misleading notices to the Employment Exchange. He cited several examples of irregularities and deception. The inefficient Labour Department of the Government was being taken for a ride. He also cited proof of corruption prevailing in the Baitarani Gramya Bank whose Manager had acted without any regard to existing rules. Even the Collector of Mayurbhanj was a party to the corruption.[68]

On 6 April 1982 Dash moved a motion in Ecology. It was a new sphere of Legislation having far reaching results and similar to the line of thinking by Scientists and Humanists all over the world. The commencement of debate on Environmental problems could be regarded as a Milestone in the career of Dash. The issue on which he spoke with authority had profound educational value besides having impact on the living species. Initiating the subject he defined Environment as 600 miles of atmosphere which surrounds the Earth beyond which is space. In the atmosphere first 5 miles consist of a thin layer which sustains life of all types and categories. He warned about the gravity of the matter saying that life would be destroyed if Environment is not protected against pollution of air, water and soil. The balance existing between these elements was to be maintained and safeguarded by all means. He was aware of the all-India debate currently going on in the country. He was equally aware of the growing public consciousness in the world and the initiative taken by several Industrialised Nations in the West and Japan. Orissa had just begun to ponder over the issue. He cited about the prevalence of a River Water Pollution Act in Orissa which had many loopholes for the offenders to avoid punishment. He, therefore, suggested for more stringent laws which would not leave scope for either Stay Order from the Court or Injunction. The Government of India had created a Department of Environment Control to implement the policies against pollution. Since Industrialisation was a major cause of river water pollution in India, Dash urged upon the fellow legislators and the Government not to allow setting up of Industries without adequate safeguard against pollution by making Anti-pollution measure a pre condition for granting license. He suggested the Government to consult an Expert Committee before introducing any legislation in the matter. He cited the action taken by the Karnatak Government as an ideal example. The Speaker of the Assembly advised the Government to take a note of what the Honourable Member (P.K. Dash) said on a matter of profound importance.

The above discussion on Environmental pollution evoked great interest among the MLAs. Some of them substantiated the fear of Dash by adding more facts and illustrations. Particular mention may be made of the participation by Haladhar Mishra, the MLA from Gandia.[69] He whole heartedly supported the motion of Dash and stated how environment was in great jeopardy. He analysed the Green House effect and its serious consequences on the living beings. The hazards of destroying forest were outlined. There was shortage of rainfall, more erosion of soil, more pollution of water and air. He appreciated the policies of the Governments in Israel and West Germany in their effectiveness to preserve the environment and create new forests to provide fresh air. Hence, the Government of Orissa was called upon to introduce necessary laws to preserve environment, create new forests, and prevent deforestation. He was in favour of having a new Department of the Government to take up these activities.[70]

In reply to the above, the Honourable Minister of State for Forest[71] (Kishore Chandra Patel) agreed with the suggestions. He assured the House to arrange a legislation after examining various aspects of the issue. With his assurance the motion of Dash was withdrawn.[72]

Dash Elected Speaker

During his long tenure as a member of the Legislative Assembly, Das had established the reputation of a very seasoned democrat who valued freedom of expression and accountability to the people. Since he was the Seniormost Member and had been elected maximum number of times to the Assembly, none deserved the position of Speaker better than him. On 22 February 1984 the Chief Minister Janakiballabh Patnaik proposed his nomination which received unanimous support in the House. He was declared elected by the Deputy Speaker, who, while making the announcement sang an eulogy on the new speaker. He recounted how Dash had been returned to the House consistently for seven times from 1952 to 1980 with one break in 1974. He praised the Speaker's undaunted character, strong personality, boldness to speak the truth and his inimitable expert knowledge on matters relating to Transport, Lift Irrigation, Forest and Agriculture. By electing him speaker the House had paid fitting tribute to a born democrat and servant of the people. He had no doubt that Dash's profound experience in the working procedure and rules of the Assembly would be a living Institution for the Legislators to learn the basic values of Parliamentary democracy.

Prasanna Kumar Dash was escorted to the Chair by the Chief Minister of Orissa and Deputy Speaker of the House. For Dash it was evidently a red letter day. From a humble Drummer in 1939 he rose to the lofty position of Speaker of the Orissa Legislative Assembly in 1984. It was the logical culmination of a dedicated career which had never witnessed any compromise of principles for self interest. Speaking high of the Speaker's personality and character, the Chief Minister wished him long fruitful life as a Parliamentarian. He was endowed with the rare qualities of a Speaker like deep insight into the views of the Opposition and understanding the constraints of the Government. None before him had served both in the Opposition Party and with the Party in Power, Patnaik had no doubt that under the stewardship of Dash, the values of Parliamentary democracy and the dignity of the House would remain safe. He expressed his gratitude to the newly elected Speaker for having upheld the rich tradition of Indian culture and wisdom through thought provoking speeches and participation in the proceedings. On behalf of the Congress Party he assured full cooperation in conducting business of the House.

Other members who spoke with emotion and fervour were Sarat Dev of Ali, Biswanath Sahu of Chhatrapur, Haladhar Mishra of Gandhia, Bipin Das of Pipili and Somnath Rath, the outgoing Speaker. In reply to the felicitations, Dash acknowledged with humility the warm greetings of the colleagues. He promised to keep up the rich tradition and legacies of illustrious persons like Lingaraj Panigrahi, Pandit Nilakantha Dash, Nandakishore Mishra etc. who had earlier adorned the Speaker's chair. He compared himself with a common man of Orissa whose only strength was popular support. He said, "I am a democrat in mind and in action" and promised to uphold the basic principles of democracy. Tolerance and respect for other's views would be the vital factors in running the business in the House. Persuasion rather than coercion, understanding rather than indifference, would be his watchwords. He would follow the path of Mahatma Gandhi and seek the blessings of Lord Jagannath in all his activities in the country. With these words he started discharging the duties of Speaker from 1984 (February).[73]

The role of the Speaker in Parliamentary democracy has been quite significant since its inception. He is elected by the Legislative Assembly and presides over its meetings. As such he occupies a position of exceptional importance. On him depends the discipline and order of the House. While imitating the British system and Institution, the founding fathers of Indian Constitution expected the Speaker to remain completely detached from partisan outlook. The Speaker is regarded as the custodian of the rights and privileges of the House. He enjoys a dignified position in democracy. According to Sir Erskin May

> "Confidence in the impartiality of the Speaker is an indispensable condition of the successful working of procedure."[74]

Lord Bryce has observed,

> "The note of the Speaker of the British House of Commons is his impartiality. xx On his way from his place on the benches to the Chair he is expected to shake off and leave behind all party ties."[75]

Austin Ogg writes,

> "Outside, no less than inside, of the House, the Speaker abstains from every appearance of partisanship. He never publicly discusses or voices an opinion on party issues; he never attends a party meeting; he has no connection with party newspapers; he never sets foot in a political club; he, of course, makes no campaign for his reelection."[76]

Munro, similarly observes,

> "The Speaker, from the moment he takes the chair, ceases to be a Party-man. xx He must act with the impartiality of a Chief Justice."[77]

Herman Finer thinks

> "He is, as near as human being can be, impartial, and that rules and practice of the House came to life without interposition of his personal or Party view."[78]

To ensure the impartiality and independence of the Speaker, the convention is to elect him unanimously and he remains in office during the life of the Legislative Assembly. If the Speaker of the preceding Assembly is elected a member of the new House, convention accepts his re-election to the Chair. The dignified role of the Speaker in conducting the business of the House depends on his impartiality. He is neither a Government's man, nor of the Opposition. Such being the ideal role of a Speaker let us examine how far Dash could follow the stipulated norm. Those who proposed and seconded his nomination or those who unanimously elected him to the coveted position in democracy had not even an iota of doubt that he would rise to the occasion fulfilling the high expectations of all and sundry.

The Speaker presides over the sittings of the Legislative Assembly and conducts its proceedings. He does not vote on any legislation unless there is an equity of votes on any particular issue. In such a situation he can exercise his casting votes. He enjoys a position of great dignity, honour and authority. Although he is the choice of the majority party in the Assembly, yet after assumption of office he is expected to function in a non-partisan manner. For his neutrality, he commands the confidence and respect of all parties in the House. He is expected to guard the freedom and liberties of the House from every possible intrusion. He not only maintains order with in the House and interprets the rules of procedure, his rulings are not subject to the jurisdiction of any Court. He is the main spokesman of the Assembly in many matters. It is his privilege to endorse a Bill as a Money Bill and his decision in the matter is final. He is the Supreme Head of all the House Committees setup by him in the Assembly. He issues directions to the Chairmen of all Committees in matters relating to their working and procedure. He is the Lord of the debates which he conducts judiciously. He ensures that members confine themselves to the issues under debate and maintain proper decorum in their speeches. His rulings on points of procedure are final. Within the above parameter of functions and privileges we have to assess the activities of Prasanna Kumar Dash during 1984 to 1990.

Dash was expected to tread upon the beaten track to keep his reputation above board. His Chairmanship career began with the Governor's Address on 23 February 1984. The Governor, as usual gave an outline of the policies and programme of the Government highlighting the priority areas to ensure development and welfare. Summarising the achievements of the Sixth Plan targets, he detailed Plan and Non-plan expenditure or Poverty eradication programme, agriculture, Irrigation, Power, Education, Forest, Animal Husbandry, Fisheries, and Urban Development. He also outlined the Government's efforts to provide employment to educated unemployed and upliftment of the poverty stricken people. The debate on vote of thanks was conducted smoothly avoiding any unpleasantness.[79]

The assassination of Smt. Indira Gandhi on 31 October 1984 led to a change of Government at the Centre with Rajiv Gandhi forming the new Council of Ministers. India headed for a mid term General election in December 1984 which gave a landslide victory to the Congress (I) Party. From Orissa the Congress candidates won in 20 Parliamentary constituencies. Only one constituency elected a non-Congress candidate to the Lok Sabha. With such unprecedented victory at the centre, the Congress High Command rightly decided to hold election in the States in March 1985. This time also the Congress Party won 117 seats under the leadership of Janaki Ballabh Patnaik who was elected as the leader of the Congress Legislature Party. Prasanna Kumar Dash contested the election from Baripada constituency. His contestants were not very formidable this time. The voters of *Purana* caste had formed a strong organisation in support of their candidate. Except this *Purana* candidate all other contestants lost their security deposit and Dash got elected with a lead of 17,000 votes from his nearest rival. This was his eighth victory and a record in the history of Assembly election in Orissa. He expected a Ministerial berth in the Council of Ministers of Janaki Ballabh Patnaik. But as he was proposed for a second tenure of Speakership his supporters were happy. His election as Speaker was unanimous. The Opposition was not very strong as the Party in power had an absolute majority. It was the presence of Biju Patnaik as the Leader of the Opposition which added new dimension to the Opposition Group. Several times the Chief Minister and the Leader of Opposition were found involved in the battle of wits and floor manipulation. That created new challenges for the speaker. There were occasions when the members of the Assembly unhesitatingly resorted to character assassination and show of physical force. These were very trying moments for a veteran like Dash whose democratic values were of a high order. Indiscipline among the Legislators·was not only unfortunate in the history of Assembly, but also quite painful to the older generation who cherished old values of dignity and exemplary behaviour. At times the question of privilege was raised on flimsy ground and had to be taken up for discussion on priority basis by the Speaker ignoring more important and serious issues of the State.[80]

The experience of Dash as Speaker of the Orissa Legislative Assembly during 1985-90 has been graphically recorded in his autobiography to provide an idea about the manner of conducting business. In the first year there were two sessions of the Assembly; the first session which lasted from July to August 1985 was relatively a smooth and pleasant one. Since Biju Patnaik was the leader of the Opposition every one expected him to show exemplary behaviour for the junior MLAs to emulate. But the second session which had to pass the Budget was a stormy one. The atmosphere was surcharged with emotion and temper running high over controversial and sensational issues like, (*i*) draught situation in Kalahandi, (*ii*) a land deal by the Chief Minister at Rameswarpur in Puri district; (*iii*) Police firing at Kakatpur; and (*iv*) Matters relating to Paradeep port. Kalahandi being a draught prone area, even the Prime Minister was keen to improve upon the existing situation. But as his personal visit to the affected areas did not make any dent on the callous attitude of the local administration, the Opposition made loud protest on the emotive issue. Adding fuel to fire the unfortunate statements of the Minister of Revenue had inflamed the Opposition anger to a climax leading to rampage in the House. For creating pandemonium and boycotting the proceedings of the House by a walkout, the Opposition was condemned by the Speaker.[81]

It was the year of centenary celebration for the Indian National Congress. There were nation wide meetings and celebrations by the Party and its leaders. Dash attended one such meeting near Kaptipada in Mayurbhanj to commemorate the activities of an ultra-nationalist named Bagha Jatin who was shot dead by the British Police in 1915. Another celebration was at Ambajoda, the venue where Sarat Chandra Das, the former Prajamandal leader and the mentor of Dash had launched the Peasant movement in 1939. Many other congregations were held subsequently to felicitate the nationalists for their sacrifice. Dash shared the platform along with other leaders like Janaki Ballabh Patnaik, Harekrushna Mahtab etc. He spoke on the history of freedom movement and the high ideals of Gandhi, Patel, Nehru and others, but did not touch upon current politics. He called upon the Congress Party not to veer away from the basic ideology and principles of the party.[82]

In 1986, the session of the Assembly began from 31 January. The Budget session which commenced from 3 March was significant. On account of some slanderous publication in the *Illustrated Weekly of India* vilifying the character of the Chief Minister there were tumultuous scenes of unrestrained behaviour in the Assembly. The Chief Minister filed a defamation suit against the Editor of the *Weekly* and through a Court Injunction prohibited any further discussion or publication on the scandalous issue. Yet the Opposition was determined to force him for resignation or else threatened to jeopardise the business in the Assembly. They wanted Dash to pressurise the Chief Minister to resign which he flatly declined to do. As the Session began on 3 September there were unprecedented scenes of disturbance. The Speaker was surrounded and threatened to be physically lifted if the session would not be adjourned. The situation was quite grave as well as unfortunate. But Dash remained firm in his decision not to adjourn the House and asked the Treasury Bench to proceed with usual business as per the Agenda. However, he observed that though the Chief Minister was present in the House he was sitting quietly and the trouble makers had not surrounded him in their scheme of thwarting the business in the House. Later on he was informed that the Opposition deliberately wanted to be expelled from the House by the Speaker so that they would glorify their own image drawing sympathy of the public. Dash conducted the business with great tact and firmness. He did not agree with the Chief Minister's suggestion to suspend some of the Opposition Members for their unruly behaviour. On the other hand, he scolded Biju Patnaik, the leader of the Opposition for his wrong strategy and unwise method of pressurising the Speaker instead of the Chief Minister to tender resignation. He expressed regret for Biju Patnaik's lack of foresight and immature leadership and the Opposition's misdirected energy. Biju Patnaik admitted of taking money not to create disturbance for Janaki Ballabh Patnaik and apologised for the misconduct of some Opposition MLAs. One such MLA was Prasanna Kumar Patsani who had occupied the Speaker's chair during disturbance and acted in a manner quite reprehensible for a Legislator.[83] A motion was brought by the Treasury bench to suspend Patsani for the session. Since this would have given undue publicity to the core issue of scandal undermining the prestige of the House, the Speaker did not allow any discussion, rather he pardoned Patsani to take away much of the wind from the sail of the Opposition. He brought the Session to its logical end and thanked the members for their cooperation and understanding. By doing this he could earn the love and respect of the House and the inevitable bitterness could be avoided by his deft handling of the provocative situation.[84]

The budget session in 1987 began from 23 February and continued upto 4 April. For passing the Supplementary budget, the Assembly met for a few days in September and October. Since the Budget session generally starts with he Address by the Governor, an unprecedented situation was created by Biju Patnaik who pretended delivering a written address without any prior information and abruptly left the House instructing his followers to start an uproar. Apart from this unusual incident, the Opposition brought an adjournment motion on the draught condition in Kalahandi and Koraput asking the Revenue Minister to pay a visit to the affected areas. That was also the desire of the House communicated through the Speaker. But the non-compliance of the ruling created an unfortunate situation when the Opposition demanded a vote on the issue and 17 Congress MLAs supported the motion. The adjournment motion brought the Infighting in the Congress Party to the open and the vote by the Dissenters created a new slur in the conduct of the Legislature. Since Kalahandi-Koraput problem frequently figured in the processings of the House, Dash was often deputing concerned Ministers to the District for an on the spot study and thereby could avoid unnecessary heat in the debate. He could also successfully handle another Adjournment motion proposed by the Opposition on the shifting of the Headquarters of South Eastern Railway from Gardenreach in Calcutta to Bhubaneswar. He had always maintained warm personal relation with the MLAs irrespective of their party affiliation and age. Therefore, when the 1987 session came to an end in October eloquent speeches were made by the stalwarts like Biju Patnaik, Rama Krushna Patnaik, Trilochan Kanungo and Prasanna Patsani etc. praising the speaker for his style of functioning which could avoid confrontation and deadlock in the House.[85]

The Budget session of 1988 commenced from 24 February and continued for long 45 days. Second Supplementary Budget session was held from 28 September to 12 October. Both the above sessions were memorable for several reasons. While the Treasury Bench made sincere efforts to place the issues concerning administration, welfare and development, the Opposition members exhibited undesirable behaviour in a bid to glorify themselves. Since the next General election was approaching fast, they devoted less and less time to discuss threadbare the pubic issues converting the Assembly to a mini battle ground to exhibit their physical strength. There was spirit of competition among the members irrespective of their party affiliation. They, unfortunately, received due encouragement from the Press. The standard and reputation of Parliamentary democracy in othgr States as well as the Lok Sabha had taken a nose dive putting the nation to shame. National freedom and dignity had become a mocking and ridiculous concept. Exhibition of Improper and unbecoming conduct by the MLAs and MPs had become utterly scornful and reprehensible. Honourable Members showed a profound lack of patience and tolerance. Maturity of mind and mutual respect had been thrown to the wind. Very often unruly members had to be suspended from the House or the House had to be adjourned. In Orissa, the Speaker had a very trying time and unenviable position in conducting business of the House amidst scenes of uproar and walkout. He could avert disciplinary action against indiscipline by his own moral forces and emotional appeal. An earlier example: on 21.9.82 Balgopal Mishra, MLA, Loisinga had misbehaved with the leader of the House by placing a shoe on his table. A motion to suspend Sri Mishra for the session was tabled by Dash.

> That this House resolves that Sri Mishra, MLA from Loisingha Assembly Constituency, No. 110 be suspended from the services of the House for the remainder of the current session for his grossly disorderly conduct derogatory to the dignity of the House and utter disregard to the rules on 21.9.82.

Including Prasanna Kumar Dash who had brought the motion many other members condemned the behaviour in very strong words. After Mishra begged to be excused and regretted for his conduct, the motion was withdrawn.[86] Not only the incident was expected to have wide repercussion on public behaviour, but also was casting a deep slur on the character of the Law makers of the country. The House and the Chief Minister were not unnecessarily worried for the incident. The views and discussion of the Members on the motion explains their hurt psyche over the moral degradation that had set in. Dash was mortified for the indirect and direct encouragement the leader of the Opposition was giving to create pandemonium in the House. The utter disrespect which some of the Opposition members showed to the Governor while he was addressing the House on 24 February 1988 caused deep anguish in the mind of Dash.[87] He saw no justification in allowing an adjournment motion on concocted and fabricated issues.[88] The behaviour of Biju Patnaik as the Leader of the Opposition had very often impeded the proceedings of the House. That had to be accepted as a *fait accompli* in our system of Parliamentary democracy in which the honourable MLAs and MPs could afford to misbehave behind the facade of legislative freedom which provided legal immunity.

Dash accepted as normal any emotional outburst on genuine problems effecting the life and future of the people. For example, corruption prevailing in the Transport

Corporation served as a genuine cause of uproarious conduct in the Assembly. Immediate response of the Government clarifying some points of order failed to pacify the agitated members. Dash had to intervene in the matter by giving specific directions to the concerned Minister which was unpalatable for the Government. The request of the Chief Minister to take a lenient view of the Minister did not yield any fruitful result because Dash espoused the principle of accountability in administration.[89]

Very often problems of the constituencies come for discussion in the Assembly and the concerned MLA takes special interest to project himself during the debate to gain publicity. The members do not hesitate to arrange a public demonstration outside the Assembly when debates are on. They even organise *"Jail-bharo"* agitations while giving anti-Government slogans to draw public sympathy. Long memorials addressed to the Government are submitted to the Speaker. Such futile exercise fail to make any dent on the Administration except that the energy of the Police (Home) Department are frittered away for maintaining law and order.

The Assembly sessions of 1989 had special significance on account of the general election scheduled for 1990. For long ten years the Congress Party was in power in Orissa. To improve their public image each party was eager to create an untoward situation in the Assembly. The Budget session began on 21 February with the Address by the Governor. As usual Biju Patnaik-led-Opposition created disturbance and walked out of the House. The entire session witnessed uproarious scenes of indiscipline on some pretext or the other. One occasion was created by the arrest of Balgopal Mishra, MLA from Loisingha by the Collector of Bolangir. Though the Speaker gave his ruling the Opposition members refused to be pacified and created pandemonium in the well of the House. Kalahandi was a perpetual cause of adjournment motion tabled by the opposition members. Trivial issues like allotment of seats in the oath taking ceremony of the new Governor at Rabindra Mandap also led to Privilege and Adjournment motion in the House. No one was prepared to see reason or refrain himself from such shameful behaviour. The important and serious matters of public concern did not receive due attention they deserved. Irrational behaviour of old, young and sundry reduced the Legislative Assembly to a mockery of play ground. On a sensational issue revealing clandestine land deal of the Chief Minister who misled the House by suppressing facts, the Opposition threw all rational behaviour to the wind. They assembled at the well of the House, snatched away papers from the Reporters, physically occupied their tables and shouted slogans. Some of the lady members of the Opposition also behaved in an improper manner. This provoked the Treasury Bench who involved themselves in scuffles and physical assault. Pradeep Maharathi, one of the main miscreants of the Opposition pretended to have lost sense and fell down. He was removed to the Hospital and the Assembly was adjourned for a day. That Maharathi was actually not injured in the scuffle and his melodrama was a mere pretension was soon confirmed by the Chief Medical Officer. Maharathi later on admitted the same before the Speaker. The support he received from other members of the Opposition was not only amazing but also unfortunate. The Assembly session which was meant to discuss the problems of the people had thus been reduced to a farce. This represented the abominable state to which Parliamentary democracy had been reduced by the honourable Legislators and the guardians of public interest.

The above deterioration could not be prevented by any moral or political force. A climax was reached on 13 September 1989 when the Opposition members started a *Dharana* (sit down demonstration) at the well of the House that continued for three days. Though they did not stall the proceedings of the House, some of them showed obnoxious behaviour like singing cheap film songs in a discordant manner which provoked laughter. They intended to be physically removed from the House to enjoy publicity, but the Speaker did not oblige them with such a ruling.

Another example of moral degradation which had set in our political life was in the form of floor crossing. Members of the Legislative Assembly invariably contest election under Party leadership. If their self interests can not be fulfilled, they feel tempted to change over to another Party with complete disregard to integrity of character and ideological affinity. One such case was that of Bhajamana Behera who after being dropped from the Council of Ministers first became a dissenting Congress member and subsequently joined the Janata Party. His case came under the Anti-Defection Act that led to his expulsion from the Membership.[90] Though Dash considered this decision as "harsh and unfortunate" he followed the existing rules in their letters and spirit.

Some Important Rulings by the Speaker[91]

The Speaker at times gives his ruling on either important or controversial issues. That bears legal implication in the context of the provisions of our Constitution. A few such rulings given by Prasanna Kumar Dash may by cited here to appreciate how efficiently he managed the business of the Assembly.

On 4 February 1986, Trilochan Kanungo raised a constitutional issue stating that there was a delay of more than six months between the session which ended on 2 August 1985 and the session which began on 31 January 1986. As such it violated the Article 174 of the Indian Constitution. The Speaker ruled that there was no violation of the Article 174 on the basis of Law Lexicon.[91A] On 12 February 1986 the Speaker gave his ruling on a submission of Bhagabata Behera, MLA. He clarified that concerned Departments submit 159 copies of the answers on submission made in a particular session to the Assembly Secretariat for distribution before the next session is convened.[92] Since his ruling was not complied with by the concern Departments, he expressed his severe displeasure on the defaulting departments. He cautioned the Departments to be prompt in future.[93] Referring to a notice on a question of Privilege against Sri Prasanna Kumar Patsani his ruling was,

> Sri Satyabhusan Shau has alleged that Sri Patsani had occupied the chair of the Speaker on the dais on 3-9-85 during the time the House was adjourned for 10 minutes due to disturbance.
>
> In the afternoon sitting of the same day I had expressed my displeasure for the actions of Sri Patsani. At the same time I had asked Sri Patsani as to the truth or otherwise of the allegation.
>
> In reply Sri Patsani has expressed his regret for the incident. In view of the expression of regret I propose that th matter may be dropped. I hope the House will agree.[94]

In the same session Sri Bhagabata Behera gave a notice on a question of privilege against Pritish Nandy, the Editor of the *Illustrated Weekly of India,* who had published some derogatory information against the character of Sri J.B. Patnaik, the Chief Minister under the caption "Some Strange Escapades of J.B. Patnaik" (May 18-24). His aim was to raise the controversial issue in the Assembly for a discussion. The speaker gave his firm ruling that since the matter was not related with the performance of the Chief Minister in the House, no discussion would be allowed and there was no breach of privilege.[95] He disallowed many privilege motions when these were found baseless or devoid of prima facie merit. Such rulings were given on the incidents of 9-11-86, 2-3-87, 5-3-87, 9-3-87, 13-3-87 and 19-3-87. This was done to save time of the House for other important matters. He disallowed privilege notices against Dr. Sradhakar Supakar (27-3-87; against the Editor, Printer and Publisher of the *Prajatantra* (28-2-87), against the Chief Editor, Editor and Publisher of the *Samvad* (10-3-87), against the Minister of Food and Civil Supplies, against the Minister of Industries (4-4-87), against the Minister, Community Development and Rural Reconstruction (20-3-87), against the Chief Minister (5-9-84), against the Minister of Finance (31-3-87) and against the Minister of State for Works (7-3-87) with convincing reasons. There were occasions when some members sought ruling of the Speaker on actions or statements made by the Chief Minister so as to create an embarrassing situation. Trilochan Kanungo raised a point of order against the Chief Minister for having made a public statement at Kotpad (27-2-88) regarding Government decision to exempt arrear loans from payment before making such a statement in the House. The Speaker made categorical statement that

> There are rulings that policy statements made outside the House without making such statements first in the House when the House is in session does not constitute breach of privilege,
>
> In this case, I may inform the House that the Chief Minister has made an announcement in the House about exemption from payment of arrear loans twice on 25-2-87 and 26-2-88.

> I refuse my consent.[96]

Kanungo brought another privilege motion against the Chief Minister for having misled the House in regard to the percentage of population below the poverty line.[97] In refusing to accept the motion the Speaker stated,

> xx I had referred the notice to Chief Minister for his clarification and, have got his reply in the meantime.
>
> The Chief Minister in his reply had enclosed a statement which was placed before the Lok Sabha dt. 11.11.87. The figures in said statement are based on 38th Round National Sample Survey relating to the period from January to December 1983.
>
> As it appears Sri Kanungo has relied on the figures of 32nd Round National Sample Survey which relates to the period from July 1977 to June 1978 where as the figures referred to by the Chief Minister are based on 38th Round National Sample Survey which relates to the period from January to December 1983. Therefore, the question of misleading the House by the Chief Minister does not arise.
>
> I refuse my consent.[98]

The rulings of Dash were often quite business like based on relevant facts, rules and precedents. There was an occasion when the MLA from Loisingha Constituency brought a Privilege motion against the Secretary, Home Department on 15th October 1987 alleging that the latter had cast aspersion against the former. The ruling on the matter was,

> xx Before I go into the merit of the case, I would invite the attention of the House to the provisions of Rule 116-C, which says that it is not permissible for a Member to deviate from or add to what he has stated in his written notice of submission. I have made a comparative study the

written notice of Sri Mishra and the speech made in the House. He has brought allegation in the House against S.P. Bolangir, about which there was no indication in his written notice and therefore, the statement made by him is not in accordance with the said rule.

Secondly, there is definite procedure for bringing allegations in the House against officials, according to which a member intending to bring allegations should first give previous notice to the Speaker and to the Minister concerned, so that the Minister could make a statement in the matter. Sri Mishra has not taken recourse to this method.

In my opinion, what Sri Mishra has stated in the House against the SP, Bolangir is not in conformity with the rules and existing Parliamentary procedure.

Rule 116C provides that the Department concerned shall reply to the submission made in the House and the requirement of the rule has been complied in the case. xx

As I have earlier pointed out Honourable members should substantiate allegations with definite proofs. Making allegation without proof and substance is against Parliamentary norms and decorum. This is what the Government have held in this case. The question of privilege, therefore, does not arise.

I refuse my consent.[99]

The rulings given by Dash were not motivated by his malice against any Individual or Institution. He was always guided by the principle of Impartiality and dignity of the House.

The proceedings reveal that some particular members were often raising points of Order, bringing adjournment and privilege motions, may be with genuine interest to get the required data on administration, or cause embarrassment or stall the proceedings temporarily. The situations created thereby had to be dealt with carefully avoiding legal complications or creating wrong precedence. Deft handling of such matters required thorough knowledge on rules of procedure and understanding the gravity of the issues raised. Dash's style of functioning had the advantage of thorough knowledge of rules of business in the House and earlier precedence in Speaker's ruling. He made debates and discussions to the point by keeping the members and the Government on the right track.

Towards the end of 1989 political clouds began to gather in Indian sky on account of the declining popularity of Rajiv Gandhi, the leader of the Congress Party and the Prime Minister. Allegations of corruption for receiving kickbacks from the Bofors Gun deal alienated his public support. His differences with Viswanath Pratap Singh, the Finance Minister culminated in the latter's resignation from the Council of Ministers and expulsion from the Congress Party. Rajiv Gandhi's Government came under sharp public criticism which generated a popular movement to keep the country free of the corrosive influence of corruption. Viswanath Pratap Singh contested from Allahabad constituency in a bye-election and got elected with overwhelming votes. The bye-election was a sort of referendum to vindicate the moral values personified by Singh. He emerged as the rallying point of the Opposition (Non-Congress) Parties of India and subsequently their undisputed leader. The Opposition Parties formed an electoral alliance in a bid to oust the Congress from power in the ensuing general election.

The general election was scheduled for November 1989. As the date of the election approached, the National Front Parties intensified their organised effort to oust the Congress

Party by nominating their candidates for straight contest in the Lok Sabha Constituencies. They could mobilise the votes of the minorities and depressed class peoples in their anti-Congress drive. People were not happy over the dictatorial style of functioning by Rajiv Gandhi. In Orissa, Biju Patnaik led the Janata Party as an election-ally of the National Front of V.P. Singh. In Orissa, the people had not been benefited by the decade long Government of the Congress. The Chief Minister's Image had suffered set back on account of his subservient attitude to Rajiv Gandhi. Growing problem of poverty caused by unemployment and lack of employment opportunity generated an anti-incumbency feeling among the voters. People again trusted Biju Patnaik's capability and dynamism. The heydays of the Congress Party in power were over. In the centre the Congress was reduced to the status of main opposition with Rajiv Gandhi as the leader. The Congress had lost its hold in states like Uttar Pradesh, Madhya Pradesh, Bihar and West Bengal. In the Lok Sabha, the Bharatiya Janata Party occupied the third position with 84 members. They supported the National Front Government of V.P. Singh. For a few years there was great instability in the Centre on account of V.P. Singh's decision to implement the Mandal Commission Report recommending more reservation advantages to the Scheduled Castes and Scheduled Tribes in job opportunities offered by the Government of India and Public Sector units. Internal dissension in the Government widened on account of the feud between V.P. Singh, the Prime Minister and Devilal, the Deputy Prime Minister. Taking this opportunity, the Bharatiya Janata Party created a controversy on the *Ram Janmabhumi* issue in Ayodhya and people's agitation against Mandal Commission Report and V.P. Singh Government's policy enhancing reservation quota to 37% intensified all over the country. The all-India scenario further got complicated due to the *Ratha Yatra* of L.K. Advani, the leader of the Bharatiya Janata Party. With the arrest of Advani by Laloo Yadav's Government in Bihar, there was withdrawal of support to the Government of V.P. Singh at the centre. His fall paved the way for a change of Government at New Delhi where Chandrasekhar's Samajvadi Janata Party came to power. He too failed in giving India a stable Government and resigned after six months due to withdrawal of support by the Congress Party. Such All-India scenario made election to the Lok Sabha inevitable. The performance of the Congress Party in the Lok Sabha election and 1989 was miserable in Orissa as only 3 candidates could win the election and the rest 19 were swept away by a strong anti-Congress wave.

In view of the miserable performance of the Congress Party in the Lok Sabha election, the Congress High Command decided to change the Chief Minister in Orissa besides appointing a President for the Pradesh Congress organisation. The High Command selected Hemanand Biswal as the new Chief Minister of Orissa while Nandini Satpathy, a former Chief Minister was appointed as the Party Chief. For divided leadership and non-performance of the corrupt Government of Patnaik, the Assembly election in Orissa held in February 1990 did not hold much promise for the Congress Party. Neither Hemanand Biswal nor Nandini Satpathy had any influence on the Orissa electorates. Biju Patnaik's Election manifesto promised loan exemption, employment, second Steel Plant and Public distribution of the ill gotten black money of Janaki Ballabh Patnaik and his former colleagues in the Council of Ministers. Biju Patnaik's dynamism could sway the voters' support in favour of the Janata Party by propaganda and tall promises. The Congress Party could win 10 seats only. In the Janata wave Prasanna Kumar Dash lost the election from Baripada constituency by a narrow margin.[100]

This was the second defeat of Dash in his public career. From 1990 to 1995 he engaged himself in organisational work and in implementing various development projects in Mayurbhanj. This phase constituted a very significant period of his life.

References

1. S. Nanda, *Coalitional Politics in Orissa,* (New Delhi, 1979), p. 69.
2. *Ibid.,* pp. 69-75.
3. Congress-31; Swatantra-49, Jana Congress-26; Socialists-23.
4. P.K. Mishra (ed), *Comprehensive History and Culture of Orissa,* Vol. II, No. 1 (New Delhi, 1997), p. 425.
5. S.N. Dwibedy, *Quest for Socialism* (New Delhi, 1984), p. 242.
6. S. Nanda, *op.cit.,* p. 148.
7. K.S. Padhy, *Corruption in Politics* (Delhi, 1986), pp. 92-98 and Mudholkar Report, Government of Orissa, (Home Department), 1970.
8. S. Nanda, *op. cit.*, p. 31.
9. P.K. Mishra, *et. al. op. cit.,* p. 428.
10. *Ibid.*, pp. 427-28.
11. P.K. Mishra, *Loc. cit.*
12. For Kenduleaf Scandal, see S. Nanda, *op. cit.,* pp. 81-82.
13. Press Note, Government of Orissa (Home), 9 October, 1968.
14. S. Nanda, *op. cit.,* p. 31.
15. By a Proclamation under Article 356 of the Constitution.
16. *The Statesman,* 25 March, 1971.
17. It was dissolved on 9 June, 1972. *The Hindustan Times,* 10 June, 1972.
18. P.K. MIshra, *et. al, op. cit.*, p. 428.
19. *Ibid.* p. 429.
20. The members earlier belonged to different parties having different ideologies.

21. See OJNO 334 of 1973 decided on 22 Octoberr 1973. The case was filed by Biju Patnaik and 73 others against the President of India.
22. *The Hindustan Times,* 3 March 1974.
23. *The Statesman,* 23 November, 1976.
24. P.K. Mishra, *et. al. op. cit.*, p. 431.
25. *Ibid.*, p. 433.
26. *Ibid.*, pp. 433-34.
27. *Loc. cit.*
28. Why Emergency? New Delhi : Government of India, Ministry of Home Affairs, 1975, p. 57.
29. Readers may refer to K.S. Padhy's *Corruption in Politics*, (Delhi, 1986) for a detailed study of the corruption cases involving the leaders of Orissa while they were in power. The monograph has copiously quoted Khanna Commission Inquiry Report and several CBI reports to highlight the ways administrative power was abused by high ranking politicians.
30. Proceedings, *Orissa Legislative Asembly,* Vol. I, No. 3 dt. 22 July 1977).
31. *Ibid.*, Vol. 4.
32. *Ibid.*, Vol. II, No. 8, p. 70
33. *Ibid.*, Vol. II, No. 11, p. 46 and 48.
34. *Ibid.*, Vol. II, No. 12, p. 55, dt. 22 September 1977.
35. *Ibid.*, 27th September, 1977.
36. *Ibid.*, Vol. II, No. 16, 28 September 1977.
37. *Ibid.*, Vol. II, No. 19, 3 October 1977.
38. *Ibid.*, Vol. III, No. 10.
39. *Ibid.*, Vol. III, No. 15, p. 42ff.
40. *Ibid.*, Vol. III, No. 16, pp. 40-41.
41. *Ibid.*, Vol. III, No. 16, pp. 40-41.
42. *Ibid.*, Vol. III, No. 22.
43. *Ibid.*, Vol. III, No. 23, p. 78ff.
44. *Ibid.*, Vol. V, No. 3, p. 60ff.

45. *Ibid.*, Vol. V, No. 10, 23 February '79.
46. *Ibid.*, Vol. V, No. 11, 27 February 1979.
47. Zubir Alam, *Emergency, Power in Indian Democracy,* New Delhi, 1987, p. 118.
48. Proceedings, *OLA,* Vol. I, No. 2, pp. 36-37, 1980.
49. *Ibid,*. Vol. I, No. 7, p. 50 date 7 July 1980.
50. Proceedings, *OLA,* Vol. II, No. 7, dt. 15 September 1980.
51. *Ibid.,* vol. II, No. 11, p. 54.
52. *Ibid.*
53. *Ibid.,* Vol. II, No. 13, p. 129.
54. *Ibid.,* Vol. II, No. 15, p. 109; 1 October 1980.
55. *Ibid.,* Vol. II, No. 17, 6 October, 1980.
56. *Ibid.,* p. 40.
57. *Ibid.,* Vol. III, No. 9.
58. *Ibid.,* Vol. IV, p. 44.
59. *Ibid.,* p. 46.
60. *Ibid.*
61. *Ibid.,* p. 76ff.
62. *Ibid.,* Vol. IV, No. 3, 23 September 1981.
63. *Ibid.,* p. 9.
64. *Ibid.,* p. 96.
65. *Ibid.,* 25 September 1981.
66. *Ibid.,* 28 September 1981.
67. *Ibid.,* pp. 114-14.
68. *Ibid.,* 16 March 1982.
69. *Ibid.,* pp. 38-39.
70. *Ibid.,* p. 39.
71. *Loc. cit.*
72. Procedings, *OLA,* 16 March 1982, p. 40.
73. *Ibid.,* 22 February 1984.
74. *Parliamentary Practice*, p. 235, Quoted in V. Grover and R.

Arora (ed), *Suppression of Opposition, Total Revolution and Emergency in India* (New Delhi, 1995), p. 129.

75. *American Commonwealth,* Vol. I, p. 140.
76. *European Governments and Politics,* p. 244.
77. *The Government of Europe,* p. 170.
78. Quoted in V. Grover and R. Arora, *op.cit.,* p. 123.
79. Proceedings, *OLA,* Vol. IX, No. 1, 23 February 1984.
80. P.K. Dash, *Autobiography in Oriya,* pp. 131-32.
81. *Ibid.,* p. 150.
82. *Ibid.,* PP. 150-51.
83. *Ibid.,* pp. 153-54.
84. *Ibid.,* p. 154.
85. *Ibid.,* pp. 176-77.
86. Proceedings, pp. 34-35 and 50-51.
87. P.K. Dash, *op. cit.,* pp. 242-43.
88. *Ibid.,* p. 243.
89. *Ibid.,* p. 245.
90. *Ibid.,* p. 269.
91. *Decisions from the Chair,* 1937-94, Monograph published by the Orissa Assembly Secretariat, 1995.

91A. Proceedings, Vol. III, 4 February 1986, pp. 49-51.

92. Proceedings 12-2-1986.
93. Proceedings, p. 71.
94. *Ibid.,* p. 72.
95. *Ibid.,* p. 111; Also see Orissa Legislative Assembly Debates, dt. 13.3.1986 p. 46.
96. *Ibid.,* p. 16.
97. *Ibid.,* p. 37.
98. *Ibid.,* pp. 37-38.
99. *Ibid.,* p. 72.
100. P.K. Dash, *op. cit.* pp. 288-89.

4

Looking Ahead

The Lok Sabha election of 1989 and the failure of the Congress Party to win a majority was a clear pointer to the results of the ensuing Assembly election in Orissa. Nandini Satpathy was the State Congress Chief. She was not well disposed toward Prasanna Kumar Dash and was reluctant to nominate him as Party candidate from Baripada constituency. When elections were held in February 1990, the Janata Government of V.P. Singh was in power at the Centre. Dash had two potential contestants in Chhatis Chandra Dhal, the Janata nominee and Kishore Dash, the Independent candidate. Both were young and enterprising. Dhal had solid support of the *Purana* caste people of Suliapada and Kishore Dash, the Independent candidate was a good speaker and had the support of the student voters. Dash lost the election to his nearest rival Chhatis Dhal. Not only Dhal had solid caste support to influence the result of voting, there was also the unfortunate anti-Party activities in the Congress. However, the defeat of Dash was a blessing in disguise for Mayurbhanj as he could devote more attention and time for the development works in the constituency and the District. These works gave him great job satisfaction apart from ensuring the socio-economic growth of the people of Mayurbhanj.[1]

Suvarnarekha Irrigation Project

The foremost contribution of Dash was the Subarnarekha major irrigation project. It has great significance in a draught prone district like Mayurbhanj where the main prop of economy is agriculture. In the British period the enlightened Princes had constructed minor irrigation projects at Balidiha and Haldia on the basis of resources available with them. They had taken step to exploit mineral resources like Iron ore by prospecting mines at Gurumohisani, Badampahar and Suleipat. After the merger of Mayurbhanj with Orissa in 1949, the State Government took no steps to develop the people's economic life through major Irrigation Projects or any other means. The people failed to derive any benefit under the much publicised Five Year Plan prorgramme. Though a tribal dominated district, Mayurbhanj did not receive any special attention to improve her economy. The agrarian condition worsened every year on account of recurring draughts and stagnation.[2]

On several occasions Dash had tried in vain to draw the attention of the Government to the miserable condition of Mayurbhanj through debates and discussions in the Legislative Assembly. He had time and again urged the Government to take care of the irrigation facilities. He was keen to have a major project sanctioned to mobilise the water resources of Suvarnarekha and Budha Balanga rivers. Minor Irrigation projects had failed to make any dent on people's economy. Hence, he exerted pressure on having a joint river project involving the Governments of Bihar, West Bengal and Orissa. Such a project harnessing the Suvarnarekha-Budha Balanga rivers would not only promote irrigation facilities, but also prevent flood in the lowlying areas of Bengal and Orissa adjacent to the sea. It was estimated to irrigate 1 lakh Hect. Acres of land in 14 Blocks of Mayurbhanj (10) and Balasore (4). Apart from this the estuary of Suvarnarekha would be free of flood havoc. Dash initiated dialogue with Balraj Madhok of the Praja Socialist Party in as early as 1968-69. He organised a peasants movement in support of the proposal. In 1979, the movement paralysed the working in the Tehsil Office at Betnoti. Finally, a tripartite agreement was concluded by the three Chief Ministers of Bihar, Orissa and West Bengal in 1979. The agreement was concluded with the knowledge of the Government of India. The share of water by the three States was unanimously agreed upon by them. They further decided to have the reservoir built at Chandil in Bihar (near Tata) and Itcha. The major canal carrying water for irrigation would flow from the anicut at Galudiha and run parallel to the river Suvarnarekha upto Balasore and Basta. The share of water available to Orissa would be used for irrigation in times of scarcity and supplement to the water reservoir at Haldia. This project was to share the destiny of atleast three lakhs of people in Orissa. Therefore, the project generated great hopes for the future of the tribals of Mayurbhanj. Even after the approval accorded by the World Bank and the Government of India with go ahead signal, the lackadaisical attitude of Orissa Government was quite unfortunate. While the Government of Bihar started excavation work for the Chandil reservoir, the inaction of Orissa Government created much scepticism in mind. However, as late as in 1987, the initial ceremony signalling the commencement of work was performed by the Chief Minister and Dash inaugurated the digging of Canal work. At that time the estimated cost of the Project was Rupees 1000 crores.

Dash personally visited the work sites in Bihar to evaluate the nature and progress and could make necessary changes for improvement in works being conducted by the Orissa Government. In 1989 a High level Committee under the Chairmanship of the Chief Minister decided to employ the local displaced people against Class IV posts in the Project. Some extra financial incentive as compensation for loss of land was also sanctioned. The local people were allowed to cultivate their fields till these were not submerged by the reservoir. But after Dash lost the election in 1990 many of these facilities were withdrawn by the Janata government and outsiders got employment through questionable means. This led to confrontation between the local people and the Project authorities which imposed the progress of work. The local people regretted for having voted against Dash in the recent election. Payment of compensation and resettlement were important works which needed expeditious disposal. According to the plan target, the Irrigation facilities for 15,000 Hectare Acres of land had to be completed by 1990 and 50,000 Hectare Acres by 1995. The Project was to be completed by 2000 A.D. Notwithstanding the above, the Government of Orissa delayed the posting of Chief Engineer and his core staff. The payment of compensation was delayed too causing great public annoyance. Observing such inaction, the World Bank declined to release the loan amount as long as the acquisition of land through payment of compensation had not been done.[3]

That the economic interest of Mayurbhanj was in utter neglect since 1949 when it merged with Orissa was evident from the fact that districts like Sambalpur, Bolangir, Keonjhar, Koraput, Balasore, Cuttack and Puri were benefitted by the execution of major, medium and minor Irrigation Projects. In comparison the tribal people of Mayurbhanj received nothing. Since 9 out of 10 constituencies in Mayurbhanj return Tribal candidates as Reserved Constituencies, they have been taken for a ride by the Government. If Suvarnarekha Project could be completed in time there was some hope of improving the lot of the people through better Irrigation and increasing production, rotation of crops and better agriculture. Whether the dream of Dash would come true or not only the future would tell.

Lift Irrigation Schemes

The constituencies of Baisinga, Morada and Baripada which elected Dash to the Orissa Assembly were having mostly agriculturists for whom annual rainfall was the only source of water for their crops. They never enjoyed the benefit of irrigation facilities. What ever minor irrigation projects were there had not been perpetual sources. The inordinate delay caused to implement Suvarnarekha-Budha Balanga projects had adversely affected the prospects of agriculture. Even medium Irrigation Projects initiated in 1971-72 took unusually long time to be completed. The Government exploited the subsoil water in many coastal districts like Cuttack, Puri, Ganjam and Balasore etc, but paid no attention to the needs of Mayurbhanj.

Dash took interest to exploit this new source of water for irrigation purpose ever since 1962 when he was returned by the Baisinga constituency. Lift Irrigation was dependent on power supply. But since rural electrification had not been given due priority to by the Government and survey of water resources had not begun, the significance of Dash's proposal could not be appreciated. Required manpower Infrastructure in Mayurbhanj was conspicuously absent. The district had only one Junior Engineer for the purpose under the administrative jurisdiction of Balasore. Balasore had two Lift Irrigation Divisions under an Executive Engineer. A Survey revealed that Budha Balanga, Gangahar, Son and Jambhira rivers had adequate subsoil water deposits. This prompted the Government to introduce Lift Irrigation in Basinga, Morada and Suliapada Blocks. Due to Dash's persistent efforts the number of Lift Irrigation points gradually increased. A new Division under an Executive Engineer was opened to conduct extensive survey and dig new Irrigation points.

In 1983 there was a severe draught situation in Suliapada, Morada, Kuliana and Betnoti Blocks. Atleast 10 Gram Panchayats were badly affected. Due to financial stringency fresh Lift Irrigation Points could not be dug. The Government showed reluctance to maintain and repair the old ones. Although the Government had created a Lift Irrigation Corporation to earn water cess, the administration was poor and top heavy. Dash was unhappy over the poor state of affairs and despite being a Congress Party MLA, threatened to go on hunger strike against the callous attitude of the Congress Government in the state. He gave a time schedule to the Government. The Chief Minister setup a Committee to look into the matter and the Committee approved of 34 new schemes for Mayurbhanj. Since Lift Irrigation Schemes were less expensive and result oriented, the efficacy of Dash's proposal received due appreciation. The Government agreed to implement more Schemes in each Block at the rate of one per 50 acres of land.[4]

Dash received cooperation of the District Administration to avail financial help for the people under the Rural Development and Tribal Development Schemes of the Government of India. The Schemes benefited the Small farmers, Marginal farmers, Tribals and Depressed Class people to improve their economy through Goat, Sheep, and Pig farming. This was imitated in many other districts of Orissa. The Lift Irrigation Corporation which sponsored Agro-Industry Schemes created new sub-divisions in Mayurbhanj to extend the advantages to more persons.

Minor Irrigation Schemes

Mayurbhanj State had a few minor Irrigation schemes with network of canal excavated in the British period. In course of time due to silting and bad maintenance the canals fell into disuse. The Orissa Government did not show much interest in either their restoration or upkeep. Several rivers and streams which have emerged from the Simlipal hills are capable of providing perennial water supply if harnessed for the purpose. But the lack of enterprise had resulted in the wastage of huge quantity of water. Consequently, the people found it difficult to combat against national calamities like draught.

The first effort of Dash was to execute the Badjor Minor Irrigation project in the Sadar Sub-division. He proposed the revival of old projects which had fallen into disuse. It was unfortunate that the MLAs of Mayurbhanj who represented as many as 9 Constituencies never put forth the need of Irrigation Project forcefully drawing the attention of the Government. Whosoever was inducted as Minister in the Government had not utilised his voice to allocate funds for the purpose. The political will being weak the sufferings of the people could not be remedied. Dash vehemently fought against this and successfully expedited the projects of Khadkei, Bankabal, Kala and Sunei. In the Sadar Subdivision he could revive the projects of Gadigan, Kandsa, Girisapal, Jhinkria, Ghagra and Gholmuhan in Morada Block and Kanimahuli, Ghadiasol, Jamsol, and Singda in Suliapada Block. In Baripada Block the only project that could be revived was San Dakoi.[5]

Flood Preventive Measure

Construction of embankments as a preventive measure against floods had been a regular feature since the Prajamandal movement started in Mayurbhanj in 1939 because the leaders taught the people in the affected areas to work for their own safety. The people showed great enthusiasm when mobilised for cooperative efforts. Construction of embankments was a part of the rural reconstruction programme. It required no financial help of the Government. The work generated a spirit of nationalism. There used to be annual floods in the Gangahar and its branch Budhi which often caused considerable damage in Balasore. Dash had organised the people of Baisinga and the adjacent area to construct an embankment on the Budhi. The successful completion of the work had given him great satisfaction besides experience for the future. With this experience he could complete the embankments in Sainkola and Badsahi Blocks. Thereby much of the cultivated lands could be saved from sand deposit caused by flood. Another important work was the completion of an embankment parallel to the river Budha Balanga near Pratappur. The embankment also served as a road for communication in the interior villages. In the Betnoti Block the embankment from Uttarpal to Khandadeuli was completed. In the Morada and Rasgovindpur Blocks similar embankments with stone shielding was completed to prevent flood of the Jambhira river. In the outskirts of Baripada town landslides caused by flood havoc in 1973 had posed a serious threat to the Babushai sector. Sixteen families had to be shifted and resettled in safe areas and parallel embankments had to be constructed to prevent further damage to the town.

Education

Although Mayurbhanj state had an enlightened monarchy in the British period, adequate development in education had not been made. The reign of Krushna Chandra Bhanjdeo (1867-1882)[6] had witnessed a modest beginning. His son and successor Sreeramchandra Bhanjdeo (1890-1912)[7] had increased the number of schools in Bahalda, Sirsa, Amarda, Kuamara and Karanjia etc. One of the impediments against the growth of education in those days was the non-availability of Oriya teachers in large number. The frequency and long spell of the Court of Wards administraion was another reason which thwarted the growth of education in Mayurbhanj. Due to the sudden death of the Rajas the State was brought under the court of wards during 1882-1890, and 1912-1924 when no step could be taken to augment educational facilities.[8] Therefore, Mayurbhanj remained backward and undeveloped. The population of Mayurbhanj consisting mostly of the tribals was another major reason for this. However, after the end of British rule these excuses had to be overcome through the efforts of the popular government. The Congress Government promised allround development of the Tribals to ensure their social progress by spreading literacy. This was a major commitment that had to be honoured through planning.

The Prajamandal leader Sarat Chandra Das who was the political mentor of Prasanna Kumar Dash had made the august beginning during 1948 when a few middle English Schools were upgraded to Secondary Schools and the first college was opened at Baripada. Dash in the capacity of an MLA was instrumental for starting 13 colleges of various categories in Baripada constituency alone. He helped in the setting up of multi disciplinary college complex at Jharpokhria. In view of its student strength and advantageous location this institution has since occupied the second position in the district. By providing Engineering, Polytechnic, Pharmaceuticals, Technical and general education the College has been drawing students from Bihar, Bengal and Orissa. Other Colleges which have been sponsored and assisted by Dash are located at Betnoti, Morada, Suliapada and Gadia. The Post Graduate Departments of MPC College at Baripada were started by his efforts. The College at Kuamara, and the shifting of the MPC College to its new Campus at Takatpur are his ideas.[9]

With regard to Secondary Schools, Dash made untiring efforts for the consolidation of High Schools at Morada, Rasgovindpur, Suliapada, Betnoti, Badshai, Khunta and Baripada. He contributed land and the ornaments of his wife for the development of Betnoti School. The Schools of Badsahi, Sialghati, Hempur, Khuntapur, Angla, Paikshahi, Dahikothi, Dhanpur, Soriskotha, Purnachandrapur, Bhinkiria and Barkand owe their development to his stewardship.[10]

The crowning achievement of Dash is in the establishment of the North Orissa University of Mayurbhanj-Keonjhar and its location at Sreeramchandravihar (Takatpur). It was after a persistent struggle of ten years that the University came into being fulfilling the long projected demand of the people. The University is expected to ensure the moral and intellectual growth of two tribal dominated districts of Orissa located close to Bengal and Bihar and to ensure the promotion of their culture.

Culture

The benevolent rulers of Mayurbhanj were great patrons of culture. Besides promoting Oriya language and culture they evinced keen interest to promote folk art. In promoting literature, publishing lexicon, organising literary seminars, establishing colleges for the growth of general, medical and technical education and above all in setting up the first Orissa University, they made significant contributions. Mayurbhanj has made profound contribution in promoting performing art called Chhau. It is a typical dance form with certain distinctive features that are practised and perfected in the numerous villages of Mayurbhanj. Maharaja Krushna Chandra (1867-1880) is known to have imported the tradition of Chhau from the neighbouring state of Sareikela (now a part of south Bihar). One of the Gurus who popularised and modernised the Chhau dance was Banamali Dash, the grandfather of Prasanna Kumar Dash. He was brought to Mayurbhanj to develop a School of Chhau dance by Maharaja Krushna Chandra. The dance as an art form witnessed its hey days of glory in the Pre-independence period. But after the abolition of Princely States in 1948, the art form languished for want of patronage. Its most uneviable phase was during 1949 to 1970 when the old artists slowly disappeared and no new aspirant with talent came forward to learn the tradition. An art form which had once upon a time received accolade from all over the world, was on the verge of being lost for ever. Two persons who revived Chhau dance are Bibekanand Patnaik, the Collector of Mayurbhanj and

Prasanna Kumar Dash, the MLA of Baripada.

Among several steps taken by Dash and Patnaik mention may be made of the restoration of village clubs through adequate financial support. Old artists received pension and the young ones were paid stipends to maintain themselves. Financial incentive attracted young boys and girls of respectable families to the clubs for regular practice. At the District and State levels zonal and regional competitions were held to encourage the artists to improve their standard. Research Scholars received grants to study the history and various aspects of the Dance form besides recording the diction and the choreography. The annual celebration was regularly organised at Baripada for two nights with Indian experts and Foreign tourists adding new dimension to the festival. The Government of Orissa liberally financed the Training School and the artists to keep the fascinating Chhau Dance alive in full glory and splendour. Chhau Dance of Mayurbhanj has attained the status of a rich folk art. Some scholars accept it as a martial art from with the belief that it originated in military camps. However, its distinctiveness is acknowledged in the style, music and themes.[11]

Cottage Industry

Mayurbhanj has a long tradition of having several cottage industries relating to the forest products. Since the district is full of hills and forests and facilities of irrigation are lacking, the tribal people and the marginal farmers have been dependent on cottage industries to supplement their income. One such industry is the production of Sabai grass and the associated products. This grass grows in the form of bushes without requiring heavy rainfall or regular water supply. It is cultivated in high lands where storage of water is not possible. Many farm lands in the Sadar sub-division are devoted to this cultivation. People make ropes of various types for various purposes and the Paper Mills also purchase in large quantities to make paper.

In course of time Sabai grass production has become a profitable business in the Betnoti Block and adjacent areas. It provides jobs and earnings to the agricultural labourers when they are free of cultivation. In recent years the Bank has started providing loans to the families who are engaged in making ropes in their spare times.

Another cottage industry that has now been mechanised is the making of disposable plates, dishes and cups with Sal leaves as raw material. Mayurbhanj has abundant Sal forests. The flower of Sal tree is used for making edible oil and the leaves are used for large scale production of disposable dishes and cups. The industry engages both old and the young alike. The tribal women and children produce these materials in large quantities and sell them in the weekly markets. In recent years the system of production has been mechanised. Betnoti is the centre of manufacturing huge quantities of Sal leaf plates and cups which are exported to many cities in India, Bangladesh and Srilanka. Dash could organise the unemployed agricultural labourers of Betnoti and the adjacent areas to earn their living by manufacturing Sabai grass and Sal leaf products. An unofficial estimate records that about 2 lakh persons are self employed in this trade. There is no need to invest heavy capital for the purpose.

Environment Protection

(i) Simlipal Biosphere

The protection of environment and ecological balance

are two major issues before us. Though both are interconnected, there are various aspects and dimensions of the issues. In course of his career as a Legislator, Dash got himself deeply involved in the protection of Simlipal forest in the early years of 1970s and raised the issue for a general debate in the Assembly seeking Government's assurance and formulation of policies to protect the Tropical Forest of Mayurbhanj.

Simlipal hills and forest is located centrally in the Mayurbhanj district between 20°17' to 22°34'N Latitude and 85°41' to 87°10' E Longitude. Its nearest township Baripada is 60 km away and is connected by an all weather metalled road to exploit tourist potentiality. The forest covered mountain occupies a unique place in the world on account of the archean system of rocks and magnetite with high water holding capacity. The soil is of rare type like red loam and laterite besides heavy clay deposits in the flat basin region. The climatic conditions are typical with temperature rising to a maximum of 41°C in May-June followed by rains upto September. In the autumn season the weather becomes cool and pleasant. The valleys in Southern part of Simlipal experience severe cold in winter with mercury falling to 5°C. In the Meghasan area one experiences severest cold in January. There is abundant flow of stream water through out the forest and the resultant humidity make the forest dense with many varieties of vegetations. The nights in the Summer season are cool. During the early part of Summer one experiences dust storms. Towards the second half of June, Monsoon sets in full vigour with thunder storms and torrential rains. Simlipal holds the key to Orissa's rainfall. The low pressure created in the Bay of Bengal while passing over Balasore strikes against the Meghasan range to cause heavy downpour. Since Orissa is situated in the same latitude as the Sahara and Arabian desert, the absence of Simlipal would have turned the Tropical forest to an arid desert landscape. The absence of Simlipal means the extension of Thar desert of India with other disastrous consequences. The Meghasan range of Simlipal not only works as the water tower of Orissa, but also influences the climatic condition of North Orissa. It saves Mayurbhanj from draught and famine condition. The rivers Budhabalanga, Gangadhar, Sona, East and West Deo, Sanjor, Palpala, Khairi, Bandhan and Salandi are fed by the water sources of Simlipal. They represent perennial sources of water. The cascading waterfalls of Barehipani and Joranda with their surrounding lush green valleys are full of beautiful natural sceneries which attract tourists in thousands every year.[13] Atleast six types of Forests have been located in Simlipal, viz. northern semi-ever gren forest, northern moist deciduous forest, dry deciduous hill forest, High level Sal forest and grassland and Savanna. The flora and fauna species have been categorised as endangered, vulnerable, threatened and rare. The floral species of Simlipal complex represent Australio-Africa-Peninsular India. The important Tree species available now are Sal, Simuli, Arjuna, Asana, Jamu, Champa, Kendu, Piasal, and Mahul. The forest is infested with shrub, club mosses, grasses and chandeliers of various coloured orchids. There are numerous medicinal plants. Out of 92 orchids found there are 20 representatives of Himalayan range and 8 of Nilgiri range.[14] Since the Simlipal forest is a treasure house of terrestrial and epiphytic orchids, the Simlipal Forest Development Corporation has setup an orchidarium at Gudigudiya, a tourist spot. There some of the threatened and rare orchids have been conserved.

The fauna of Simlipal significantly includes Indian elephant, tiger, bear, panther, wild boar, gaur, Asiatic wolf and deer, sambhar, four horned antelope etc. Besides the above, one finds the Hill Mayna which can imitate human voice. There are about 233 species of birds. From anthropological point of view Simlipal carries special attraction as the habitat of several primitive tribes viz., Santal, Bhumija, Bathudi, Gond, Bhuiyan, Mahali, Saunti, Ho, Kharia, Mankidia, Erenga and Sabara etc. They live on forest products like honey, seasonal fruits, roots, and trade on commodities such as Sal resin, arrowroot, mushrooms, firewood, timber and edible fruits.[15]

Unfortunately, such a beautiful place created by Nature is being systematically and ruthlessly destroyed since India's independence in 1947 on account of inefficient administration and defective management of forest wealth. Free grazing of cattle, reckless cutting of trees, shifting cultivation and fire, *Akhanda Shikar* or mass hunting by the tribals, poaching by unscrupulous traders have created irreparable damage to the virgin forest wealth. Both flora and fauna have been ransacked in the name of Tourism. Deforestation has been going faster than afforestation. This type of vandalism has seriously affected the ecology. Dash raised the first voice of protest against the depredation in the Legislative Assembly in 1972.

Dash compared Simlipal with the Himalayas which had caused monsoon rains in a vast area of Orissa, Bengal and Bihar. In his opinion, the Meghasani area having an average rainfall of 1600 mm was comparable with Cherapunji. This rainfall had promoted the growth of impenetrable Sal forest in an area covering about 3000 square kilometres. None had appreciated the value of Simlipal more than Dash. He wanted this precious gift of

Nature to be carefully preserved for the benefit of mankind. The fact that large-scale deforestation in Kalahandi and Bolangir in the Post-1948 period had turned these two erstwhile Princely States to arid lands vulnerable to severe draught situation was well known to him. He was apprehensive lest the same thing would happen in Mayurbhanj. In his speeches and writings he extolled the judicious nature of Forest administration in the Darbar regime and made scathing criticism of the inefficiency of the Orissa Government.[16] He felt deeply mortified for the deceptive policy of the Forest Department in the name of scientific management of forest wealth. He cited how during 1978-79 the Simlipal Forest Development Corporation had ruthlessly exploited the wealth of 2700 sq. kms. The Corporation's business deal was suicidal for the future of mankind. The authorities took no steps to implement the scheme of afforestation. He alleged that the Non-Congress Government (1977-80) had adopted suicidal policies being mislead by their Chief Secretary's Report.[17]

After being elected to the Assembly in 1980 Dash took up the conservation of Simlipali forest in great earnest. He created an awareness about the Dooms day by his speeches, writing and dialogues. In 1980 he brought forward non-official resolution in the form of a Bill which received wide support from other members. The Government saw the wisdom of Dash's Resolution to prohibit the felling of trees in Simlipal.[18] He urged upon the Government to resettle the inhabitants of 36 villages located in the National Park area in order to prevent regular destruction. He blamed the top heavy administration of the Corporation as a liability for the State. It was rightly predicted that deforestation would cause tornado instead of rains. His terse warning to the Government was that

Orissa would be destroyed if the growing ecological imbalance was further precipitated. Though the Minister of Forest at that time was an MLA of Mayurbhanj, Dash doubted if the Minister had ever visited Simlipal. He saw no reason why the Government of Orissa was not unanimous with the UNESCO in preserving Simlipal. He then moved the motion to constitute a House Committee[19] and the motion was approved. The House Committee was first of its kind in the history of Orissa Legislative Assembly.[20] It was supposed to act as an Advisory Committee for the Government.

Subsequently, the name of the House Committee was changed to Orissa State Environment Protection Committee with added responsibilities and wider powers. However, the above mentioned House Committee visited Mayurbhanj to gain first hand knowledge about Simlipali and few other National Parks in the country to make positive recommendations to the Government. As a result of the Committee Report, the felling of trees was stopped notwithstanding the financial loss it inflicted on the Corporation. Apart from the loss in income, Dash observed that the goal of preserving the pristine character of Simlipal was not possible on account of the simultaneous operation of three Departments in the same area with overlapping powers and responsibilities. These Departments were: the State Forest Department, the Tiger Protection Project and the Development Corporation. But nothing could be done about it.

The Tiger Project was established in 1973 to preserve the faunal species of Simlipal. In 1979 the Government declared Simlipal as a National Game Sanctuary. At Ramtirtha near Jashipur, the Mugger Conservation Centre was established. There are certain stipulated rules and regulations governing the management and objectives of a National Park, Game Sanctuaries and Biosphere Reserves laid down by the CNPPA (Commission on National Parks and Protected Areas). This is an International body forming a part of the IUCN (International Union for Conservation of Nature) and Natural Resources. Certain rules have been laid down by the Wild Life Protection Act of 1972 too. As per the provisions of this Act, in a National Park no exploitation of forest resources is permitted. The area will be out of bound for grazing of cattle and nc individual can have any building asset inside.

> The area should perpetuate in a natural state, preserving samples of physiographic regions, biotic communities and genetic resources and species in danger of exploitation, to provide ecological stability and diversity.[21]

In 1972 the Conference of World leaders held at Stockholm in Sweden first created the awareness for the protection of environment. The wave started blowing in India after 1980. The House Committees for Simlipal and Environment submitted interim Reports to the Speaker of the Assembly on 29 September 1982 and 15 September 1984. In 1985 for the first time the demand for recognising Simlipal as a 'Biosphere' was mooted. At that time India had 14 Biospheres. The Environment Conference held at Baripada and several workshops held in Simlipal, finally declared that Simlipal be acknowledged as a biosphere for its protection. The concept of biosphere intended the conservation of representative ecosystems. Its basic idea is to conserve the natural areas and the genetic material they contain. This was recommended by a panel of UNESCO sponsored programme named 'Man and Biosphere' (MAB) in 1973. The concept stipulated that the conservation of biological diversities of the forest, the genetic diversities of cultivated crops and domesticated animals need a planned and scientific Biosphere Reserve Programme. In brief, it may be said that Biosphere reserves serve the purpose of the healthy aspects of the entire biological community. The concept envisages the whole biosphere ecosystem for preservation. In managing a biosphere the responsibility is entrusted not upon Man, but upon Nature. To create a biosphere, three zones or areas are required. These are the core area, the buffer zone and the Transition area. The core area is totally protected; in the Buffer zone Tourism, recreation, research and environmental training are allowed; and the Transition area is used for research, exploitation, habitation of human beings and sustainable resource development.[22]

The Baripada Conference in 1985 attended by the Chief Minister of Orissa and the Minister of Forest and Environment of the Government of India, resolved that despite the loss of annual revenue of Rupees 5 crores, Simlipal be given the status of a Biosphere. Since then Dash as the Speaker of Orissa Legislative Assembly continued a sustained effort untiringly in this regard. The Orissa Environment Society under his Chairmanship wrote to the Government of Orissa, Government of India, UNEP and the UNESCO to accord recognition. The matter was discussed in the Assembly time and again. A high level meeting held under the Chairmanship of the Chief Minister on 23 March 1986 resolved to keep entire Simlipal under one authority to be named as 'Simlipal Development Authority for better conservation. The Orissa Government submitted the UNESCO nomination form to the Government of India in 1994 for the establishment of a biosphere reserve. A reminder was sent in the following year to expedite decision. In the meantime Dash and the

Environment Society held several meetings in and around Simlipal forest to intensify people's awareness. They also set up Environment units in about 150 villages of Mayurbhanj. Official and unofficial pressure on the Government of India steadily mounted. The prolonged efforts and correspondence in this regard can be appreciated from a few letters reproduced by Dash in his Autobiography.[23] Finally, his efforts bore fruit in 1994 when the Division of Ecological Science of the UNESCO approved Simlipal as a Biosphere with effect from 22 June (1994).[24] It was an extraordinary achievement of Dash aimed to cause benefit to a vast region of Eastern India and the people living there.

(ii) Protection of the Eco-system

As discussed earlier, the United Nations Conference on Human Environment held at Stockholm in 1972 was a milestone in the history of creating awareness to preserve the eco-system. The study and preservation of the eco-system has become essential in the context of ever growing human population, ever decreasing natural resources which sustain life. Soil, water and air are basic essentials on which survival of the living species depend. The living human species require more space, more oxygen, more food and water for which they are destroying forests and exploiting mineral and water resources indiscreetly. Industrial development has caused large scale depletion of natural resources. A century ago there was a balance maintained between the abiotic and biotic components. The destruction of the balance caused by human vandalism has brought many undesirable changes in the ecosystem. One major change that concern s the living beings is the rapid conversion of a 'Hospitable Earth' to an 'Inhospitable' one.

This change has jeopardised the existence of man, animals, birds and the plants. The fine balance existing between the physical and biological resources called Environment is under great threat precipitating the advent of the Dooms day.

The Stockholm Conference touched the alarm signal all over the world urging upon the leaders and the governments not to precipitate the process of destruction. Many international agencies like the UNEP, the WWF emerged under the UNESCO. In India the department of Environment Protection and Prevention and the Board for Control of Pollution came into being. Some efforts were made to conserve the Eco system through Non-Government organisations too.

The movement on preservation of Eco-system has made great progress in Orissa since the creation of the Department of Environment in 1982. To prevent industrial pollution the State Prevention and control of Pollution Board was created. The House Committee referred to in the preceding pages and the State Environment Pollution Council were two advisary bodies. Subsequently, many Non-Government Organisations were setup. There is a long list of these NGO units, viz. Orissa Environment Conscious Society, Nature and Wildlife Conservation Society, Briksh O Jeevara Bandhu, Society for Development Action, Centre for Youth and Social Development, Ganatantrika Adhikar Suraksha Samiti, National Institute for Participatory Action and Development Training, Peoples' Institute of Participatory Action and Research, United Artists Association, Agragami, and Gram Vikash etc. etc. These NGOs carry on the movement launched for protection of the eco-system. They conduct protests, demonstration, meetings, workshops, seminars, whenever they notice any threat against environment due to construction of dams, industries, destruction of forests, etc.

The pioneer of the above movement in Orissa was Prasanna Kumar Dash. In a marathon speech delivered in the Assembly on 7 April 1982[25] he moved the motion against Environmental pollution striking the first note of concern. Though it was a far cry in the wilderness, he spoke with conviction and courage defining—Ecology, Environmental pollution and the hazards confronting the mankind. He explained how the eco system connected earth, water, air, light, all types of living beings, rivers, sea, forest, hills, sun, moon and the stars in a delicate but immaculate fabric which if disturbed would destroy the creation due to drastic changes in the sea and landmass. Since man is superior to all other living beings the preservation of the creation solely rested on him. Quoting Mahatma Gandhi, he said,

> The earth has enough for every one's need, but not for every one's greed.

He also quoted the statement of Smt. Indira Gandhi which runs as:

> One cannot be truly human, civilised, unless one looks upon not only all his fellow men, but also all the creation with the eyes of a fraid.

With thorough knowledge, he highlighted upon the far reaching consequences of deforestation, the Green House effect and the depletion of Ozone layer. Like many scientists, he predicted deluge in the middle of the twenty-first century if the indiscriminate behaviour of man was not halted. He quoted Sanskrit texts to add weightage to his arguments and cited statistics to prove the rate at which forest wealth was being squandered.[26] Referring to the famous Rio conference in which the Ecology-Experts of 165 countries alongwith 40-50,000 representatives and Heads of States of 46 countries were present, he short listed their resolutions relating to Agenda-21 on Safety of Green House and Climatic Changes. They created a common fund to keep the Eco system free from pollution and to protect the land covered by existing forests. They made a last bid to save the planet earth from total destruction. The Conference repeatedly heard from world famous Ecologists like Dr. Brown of the USA and Dr. Srivastav of India, that by the middle of the Twentyfirst century there would be unprecedented climatic change due to increase of heat in the atmosphere caused by pollution, leading to submersion of the sea coast areas. This havoc would be added by volcanic eruptions and earthquakes. He urged upon the Government and the people to preserve the ecosystem at any cost in order to prevent total destruction of mankind.[27] That was the latest challenge posed by mother earth to the right thinking men of our time.

Dash did not agree that economic development linked to industrial growth was contradictory to environment protection. Both are equally important for the developing nations. In their natural euphoria for economic progress the western countries however, had failed to realise the evil consequences of Industrialisation. Having realised that, they have now consistently adopted measures to check pollution. These anti-pollution measures have been quite successful in West European countries, Japan and the USA, without however, diminishing their Industrial superiority. Dash believed that a developing country like India should try to emulate the above countries. He pleaded for introducing stringent legislation as a deterrent against industrial pollution. He held the Rio-Resolution to protect existing forests as binding on the Governments and sacrosanct for the people. To him population explosion, various nuclear tests and experiments conducted on land, in the Sea and air, emission of carbondioxide from vehicles, and increase of industries are as reprehensible as the destruction of forests. Concluding his discussion, Das observed that Simlipal biosphere holds the key to our survival. The above message was followed by several speeches and writings on various occasions giving him a rightful place among the leading environmentalists of our country who look much ahead of their times.

Like the Simlipal biosphere Project, Dash has left his imprint on preserving the ecosystem of Chilka lagoon which is considered as the pride of our wetland heritage. During the tenure as the Minister of Science, Technology and Environment (1995-99) he tried to prevent the silting up of the lake by positive action despite opposition of vested interests. Chilka lake is the largest brackish water lagoon of Asia situated on the East coast of Indian peninsula. It lies between 19°30'-19°57'N Latitude and 85°5'20"-85°'20" E Longitude extending from Bhusandpur in Puri district to Malud in Ganjam. It covers an area of 1055 sq. kms. The lake contains a few hillocks which provide shelter and nesting place to many exotic birds in the winter season. Its depth varies from 1.73 to 3.7 metres. The mouth of the lake which joins with the Bay of Bengal is known as Magarmukha lies almost at the central part. Several rivers like Daya, Nuna, Ratnachirc, Bhargabi and Kania deliver their fresh water from the north, and the central part receives water from the rivers Malaguni, Dhanua and Salia. From July to December the lake water gets sweeter and from December to July gets salty. By this one finds the Lake water maintains a sweet saline environment. From January onwards the sea water from the Bay of Bengal enters to the lake through its mouth Magarmukha during hightides. This creates the saline water ecosystem for about 6 months a year. Otherwise, from the July to December the water remains sweet or less saline due to the discharge of flood water from the rivers.[23]

The extraordinary feature of Chilka is that it contains 352 angiospermic species. Experts have noticed three categories of vegetation. (a) acquatic vegetation, (b) littoral scrab jungles, and (c) psamophytic vegetation. The fauna of the lake includes over 150 species of first out of which 32% are acquatic, 22% are waders and 46% are terrestrial. The migratory character of these birds is the most interesting feature.[29] The lake being a store house of many varieties of fishes provides ideal facilities for pisciculture too.

But the lake is now threatened in several ways. It is being silted up at a very fast rate because of the rivers which discharge their flood water carrying several million tons of silt every year. This has resulted in making the lake shallow and turbid. Industries set up close to the lake (Jayashree Chemicals in Ganjam) discharge their pollution killing marine species. The Naval Training centre at Balugan has added to the pollution process by discharging fuel from the boats and training ships. In addition, the poachers have been threatening the migratory birds by indiscriminate poaching. Another source of threat is posed by unscrupulous persons engaged in prawn culture.

However, the foremost problem facing the life of the lake is rapid rate of silting. This not only makes the lake shallow, but also threatens the entry point of sea water at Magarmukha. To save Chilka from extinction Dash had to appoint a suitable person who had the requisite expertise and dynamism. He saved Chilka against heavy odds. Necessary financial support came from the Government of India. Dredgers were purchased and operations began to clear the entry point. The progress was reviewed and found quite satisfactory. During his tenure as Minister, the initial impediments were removed to save Chilka from disaster. But when the first phase of operation ended with success in 1999, Dash was dropped from the Council of Ministers in February. This created a jolt in the progress of work in Chilka lake and disappointed many experts on Ecology who had expected several other measures to be adopted for Environmental protection.[30]

Notwithstanding the brief tenure as a Minister, Dash could make his mark in the field of Ecology. What ever good measures he adopted had their long term impact on environment. That may be considered his achievement as a selfless dedicated worker and his legacy for the posterity.

References

1. P.K. Dash, *Autobiography,* (Oriya) pp. 289-90.
2. *Ibid.*, p. 293.
3. *Ibid.*, pp. 295-96.
4. *Ibid.*, p. 306.
5. *Ibid.*, p. 308.
6. D.M. Praharaj, *Tribal Movements and Political History of India* (New Delhi, 1988), p. 17.
7. *Ibid.*, p. 80ff.
8. *Ibid.*, p. 85ff.
9. *Autobiography,* p. 314.

10. *Ibid.*, p. 315.
11. For further details see (*i*) K.C. Biswal, *An Introduction to the Chhau Dance of Mayurbhanj,* Baripada, 1998; (*ii*) Sitakanta Mahapatra (ed) *Chhau Dance of Mayurbhanj,* Cuttack, 1993.
12. *Autobiography,* pp. 317-19.
13. S.N. Patra (ed), *Environmental Conservation Movements in Orissa,* 1993, pp. 6-7.
14. *Ibid.*, pp. 7-8.
15. *Ibid.*, p. 9.
16. *Proceedings,* Vol. III, No. 23, p. 78ff. 1977; *Autobiography,* p. 299.
17. *Ibid.*, pp. 299-300.
18. *Proceedings,* Vol. II, No. 17, 6 October 1980).
19. *Ibid.*, Vol. III, No. 9; 9 March 1981 with 12 members under the Chairmanship of the Speaker to evaluate the problem.
20. *Autobiography,* p. 301.
21. S. Patra, *op. cit., p. 10.*
22. *Ibid.*, p. 10.
23. *Ibid.*, pp. 321-28.
24. S. Patra, *op. cit.*, p. 320.
25. See the Proceedings.
26. *Ibid.* and also *Autobiography,* pp. 328-31.
27. *Loc. cit.*
28. S. Patra, *op. cit.* p. 2.
29. *Ibid.*, pp. 3-4.
30. Supplement to Autobiography, in Press.

5

Dropping the Pilot

The election result of 1995 went in favour of Prasanna Kumar Dash who was returned to the Assembly from Baripada constituency despite sabotage activities of some leading members of the District Congress organisation. This election success being a record ninth time, gave him immense satisfaction and glory. The care that he had shown in nourishing the constituency and the district was finally vindicated. He was inducted as a Cabinet Minister by Janaki Ballabh Patnaik on 20 March, 1995 with the portfolios of Science, Technology and Environment.

During 1996-97 the Congress Party organised the celebration of Fifty Years of India's Independence in great eclat to highlight the contributions of Congress stalwarts in the struggle for freedom and the achievements made under Congress leadership since 1947. The State Government where Congress was the ruling party, had special reasons to be boastful. One of the reasons was to use the celebration as an occasion to endear themselves to the people they governed. The occasion provided equal opportunities to eulogise success as well as to introspect on failures. Many leaders urged upon their compatriots for a soul searching exercise. Official and non-official organisations sponsored a national debate as to what India had achieved during the past 50 years. The proceedings of the Orissa Legislative Assembly record some landmark speeches by a few members. One such speech was delivered by Prasanna Kumar Dash, on 18 November 1996. His reflections projected the inner thoughts and feelings of the cross section of Indian people. The quintessence of the speech was the release of pent-up emotions of a veteran nationalist and a seasoned Legislator who felt perturbed at the steady deterioration of moral integrity and social values. The speech deserves an in-depth study for full appreciation.

Dash recollected the Pre-1947 period when as a young man he had plunged into freedom movement without knowing either the implication or the results. He had merely responded to the clarion call of Sarat Chandra Das, a staunch follower of Mahatma Gandhi and a champion of the village reconstruction programme. Claiming the privilege of a senior member of the Assembly in 1996 he asked the colleagues to summarise their contributions to the country. The nationalists had pledged to redeem the country from foreign rule, to safeguard India's glorious history and cultural heritage, to improve the economy, to end exploitation and remove corruption and to give enough food and pure drinking water to the people. What was their achievement, he asked. Had the goal been achieved? A few years after, there would be a new Assembly with new generation of legislators in a new millennium. What would be the message of the outgoing Assembly for the next generation? What values would they be asked to emulate? These soul searching questions were raised before the full Assembly which had met to evaluate country's progress.

Dash cited the expectations of Swami Vivekanand that with independence, India would regain her lost cultural tradition and humane values. India had a rich tradition of Democracy, the basic feature of which was 'Tolerance'. The culture of India was based on tolerance and mutual respect. She believed in the lofty ideal of sacrifice, not enjoyment. The whole world was treated as a family. Where have these inspiring ideals and values gone?—asked Dash with an agonising mind. His observations on the contemporary events were distressful. India had strayed away from the path of Nonviolence soon after achieving independence. Man had become selfish and self centred and his goal was materialistic. To achieve his goal he had far excelled others in rampant corruption. The Ministers, Prime Ministers, Legislators, Judges and Governors who were supposed to be the guardians of public morals were steeped in corrupt practices and hauled up by the Court as Criminal offenders. Yet, they could not be punished due to the cumbersome procedure of laws. Legal lacunae was another unfortunate thing, lamented Dash. He considered political interference on Judiciary as reprehensible. There was a perceptible decline in our moral values since 1960-61 and the sacrifice of the freedom fighters were sadly forgotten. Plan targets could not be reached; the literacy drive could not be successfully implemented; an unholy nexus between the Politicians and bureaucrats had spelt disastrous results in the tenor of administration; the bureaucracy conspicuously lacked a spirit of commitment; the Ministers were devoid of a sense of accountability, and people became more right conscious without being dutiful. Such was the state of affairs in independent India, Dash said sorrowfully. The rate at which addiction to liquor and drugs had spread created consternation in his mind. The future of Indian youth was dark. Those who cherished values in the past forgot to preach for the benefit of others. Apostles of Parliamentary democracy practised political horse trading to retain power. He phoophooed the suggestion made by the Leader of the Opposition to introduce election reforms condemning the idea as vague and futile exercise. The only Reform he thought of having a salutary effect in Indian democratic setup was to make elections free of corruption. He ridiculed the practice of observing Independence Day on 15th August and Republic Day on 26 January with the help of students. It was a fact that the students constituted the audience, they paraded and saluted the National Flag before the VIP and they alone formed the spectators. People of any area in particular and those of the country as a whole were indifferent to the significance of the above two occasions. The Government and the people have drifted away from each other. He felt the absence of any administration in the country and aptly remarked that India was being governed by the judiciary through the method of "Judicial activism". His message for the 21st century was a clubbing together of all political parties in India, forging together of a strong united group, dedicated to do maximum good to the country and its people.

The historic speech of Dash had a note of pragmatism and hope. Though difficult to achieve, he expected that a new order would emerge if his countrymen would be united and patriotic. Corruption based on greed and self interest must be shunned.

But it soon became evident that Dash had lost grip on the grim realities of political life in Orissa. He himself abhorred corruption in public life; lived the life of austerity and deprivation; fervently preached a way of life which had become obsolete and anathema in politics. Remaining few years in the Government as a Cabinet Minister would show gradually how he found himself completely out of tune in a group of corrupt power hungry politicians. None paid any heed to his advice, much less admiring him for his Cassandra like predictions.

Dash received the first shock treatment at the time of assuming charge of the portfolios allotted to him. For the first time, Forest and Environment departments were separated to be handled by two different Ministers. Notwithstanding his predilections to preserve the Natural forests of Orissa and missionary zeal to safeguard the Environment, Dash was not given the Department of Forest to take care of. This deprived him from the opportunity of making Simlipal a full-fledged Biosphere. He was of course aware of his 'old age' and the difficulties in managing the Forest Department politically by warding off vested interests. However, on the ground of expediency, Forest, an integral feature of Environment, was excised and the 'Wings of Dash were clipped'. The clandestine manner in which the interest of the Party was placed before the interest of mankind deeply mortified Dash. In several public forum he gave vent to his feelings in no uncertain terms.

While the Congress Party was in power, Dash never hesitated to call a 'spade a spade'. He always maintained a clear conscience far above any self interest. Though a disciplined soldier of the Party, he could not compromise the principles and values which he had cherished in life. This led to the widening of rift between him and the Chief Minister. He analysed the incidents of misunderstanding dispassionately to arrive at some conclusions. The publication of *Karmir Sadhana* (his autobiography in Oriya) in August 1997 containing some information on the inside stories of the Congress Government of Janaki Ballabh Patnaik had appeared unpalatable to the Chief Minister. In the selection and appointment of a chairman for the State Pollution Control Board there was hide and seek game between the Chief Minister and Dash who was holding the charge of the Department. So also in implementing the policy to protect Chilka lake, a healthy understanding between the two was lacking. The establishment of North Orissa University was yet another issue which strained their relations. The Mohanty Committee appointed for the purpose, had suggested mini University Centres in the districts of Mayurbhanj, Keonjhar, Balasore and Bhadrak besides recommending Baripada as the location of main office. Though this was acceptable to the people as a whole, the Government neither accepted the proposal nor came out with any other reasonable solution. Dash was very much in favour of having the University headquarters at Baripada as a crowning achievement of his sustained effort, but felt disappointed at the procrastinating attitude of the Chief Minister. The issue could not be conclusively decided as long as J.B. Patnaik was in power. Patnaik's dilatoriness was both irritating and frustrating for Dash, apart from causing public resentment.

Among other causes which widened the rift, mention may be made about the Government's connivance with the Timber Mafias in felling precious trees in Simlipal forest for export to Bengal, Bihar and other states. Notwithstanding Dash's repeated request and warning, the Chief Minister did nothing to prevent illegal felling and selling of trees from the core areas of the biosphere. The timber mafias having been granted political blessing could operate freely with impunity. Dash had suggested the Forest area to be handed over to the Central Reserve Police Force (CRPF) for protection and the corrupt officers be transferred forthwith. To Dash Simlipal was a sacred gift of the Nature and he spent many sleepless nights worrying about its safety. The spectre of a vast region turning into desert condition incessantly haunted his mind. If the Chief Minister had political constraints to deplete Simlipal without an iota of moral compunction, Dash had equally strong emotional attachment and concern for the biosphere region. The former was motivated by greed, whereas the latter by love for the future of mankind.

On the ecology front, the establishment of a medium class port at Dhamra emerged as another contentious issue. The proposed port was to be setup at the estuary of the river Baitarani in Bhadrak district with the collaboration of a foreign company. In the context of safety of the coastal area, the existing rules had prohibited any construction within 500 metres of the sea coast. Since the Orissa Government had laid the foundation of the port in violation of the above stipulation and had not obtained prior permission of the Government of India, the prospect of the port became a bleak. The State Environment Department (under Dash) declined to give their postfacto clearance as a pre-requisite to approach the Government of India. The Chief Minister naturally felt annoyed. Dash acted as per his conscience within the framework of rules, but thereby he singed the beard of the Government. Dhamra remained the ill-fated still born baby of the Chief Minister.

On a few occasions the views of Dash were ignored by the Chief Minister. The posting of R.M. Senapati as Principal Secretary in the Ministry under Dash was one such example. Senapati's style of functioning and management was not only irksome but also injurious and provocative. The desire of Dash to get rid of him through the Chief Minister did not receive that much of weightage which it deserved. So was also the case of the Civil Supply Officer of Mayurbhanj who received political protection of the Chief Minister and could not be transferred despite serious charges of inefficiency and criminal negligence. Though in the administration of Simlipal Forest region indiscriminate felling of trees and their pilferage through Mayurbhanj-Bengal border in connivance of the Divisional Forest Officer and Minister of Forest and serious allegations of corruption were brought to the notice of the Chief Minister, but no remedial measures were taken. The value of the smuggled timber was estimated to be Rupees 38 Crores. Not only the State Exchequer suffered such colossal loss of revenue, but the depletion of the Biosphere threatened the environment as never before. The excision of the Electronics section from the Department of Dash and its transfer to the Industries Department, was like the proverbial last nail in the coffin. Without Dash's knowledge the notification for such transfer was issued assigning no reason for the decision. This was an ominous sign of approaching bad days in future.

The last few months of 1998 was a traumatic period for the Government of Janaki Ballabh Patnaik whose close friend Indrajit Roy, the Advocate General of Orissa charged of moral turpitude brought the Government under clouds of public fury. The Anjana Misra rape case of December, further aggravated the crisis, stigmatizing Patnaik's Government for its inept handling of the incident. Finally, the dastardly killing of the Australian Missionary Graham Steward Staines and his two sons at Manoharpur in Keonjhar district in January 1999 brought down the

Government of Patnaik on grounds of moral responsibility. The Congress High Command asked Patnaik to step down from office. Sri Giridhar Gomango, a sitting Tribal M.P. from Koraput and a trustworthy person of the Congress President, was elected Leader of the Congress Legislature Party at Bhubaneswar. The merit of selecting Gomango was altogether a different question. The new Council of Ministers sworn in under his leadership excluded twelve former Ministers of Patnaik's Cabinet. Prasanna Kumar Dash was one among them. His long political career, vast experience as a Legislator, honesty, integrity, and truthfulness, non-partisan attitude as the former speaker, deep love for preserving the Environment, and genuine concern for the coming generation of Twentyfirst century were thrown to the winds. The man who had personified value based politics, and austerity in public life was considered an anachronism in today's politics and government of rampant corruption and unscrupulous behaviour.

Glossary

Akhanda Shikar	Free Hunting
Begari	Carrying Luggages Free
Bethi	Free and Forced Labour
Chhau, Chhow	A folk dance
Dharana	Protest agitation
Durga Puja	Worship of Goddess Durga, A Festival
Garibi Hatao	To eradicate poverty; A catchy slogan given by Indira Gandhi
Holi	A Festival
Jail Bharo	Filling the Prisons
Jagir	Rent Free Land
Karana	A Caste
Kheda	An Operation to catch wild elephants
Kisan	Peasant
Lakhrajdar	Landlord of free holding
Magan	Forced Levy
Mahajan	Moneylender, Shopkeeper

Paik Jagir	Rent free holdings of the Paiks
Palataka	One who runs away; absconder
Pargana	Revenue unit
Pargana Samiti	A committee
Paye	A measuring container
Payeka Pancha	A levy
Podhu	A type of cultivation by clearing forest
Prajasabha	An assembly of people's representatives
Pradhan	Revenue Collector
Purana	A Caste, Peasant Class
Rasad	Free Camp arrangement
Ram Janmabhumi	Birth place of God Rama
Sarbarakar	Revenue Officer
Sardar	Revenue Collector
Satyagrahis	Those who agitate by non-violent demonstration
Shikarbethi	Levy for hunting
Tahasildar	Revenue Officer

Bibliography

Bailey, F.G., *Politics and Social Change—Orissa,* University of California Press, Berkeley, 1963.

Bambas, A.P., *Citizen's Grievances and Administration,* New Delhi, 1969.

Baral, J.K. (ed.), *Government and Politics in Orissa.*

Beard, Edmund and Stephen Horn, *Congressional Ethics, The View from the House,* Washington DC, 1975.

Benedict, Costa, *India's Socialist Princes and Garibi Hatao,* Kalyani Publishers, Ludhiana, 1973.

Bentley, Arthur, *The Process of Government, A Study of Social Pressures,* OUP, 1908.

Bhargava, G.S., *India's Watergate, A Study of Political Corruption in India,* New Delhi 1974.

Das, M.N., *Sidelights on Orissan History and Culture,* Bhubaneswar, 1978.

Dash, Nilakantha Pandit, *Autobiography* (in Oriya), Cuttack, 1996.

Dash, S.C., *Orissa, States of Our Union,* Cuttack, 1968.

Desai, Morarji, *A Minister and His Responsibilities,* New Delhi, 1970.

Dwibedi, Surendra Nath, *The Orissa Affair and the CBI Inquiry,* Cuttack, 1965.

Dwibedi, Surendra Nath, *Quest for Socialism,* New Delhi, 1984.

Dwibedi, S.N. and Bhargava, G.S., *Political Corruption in India*, New Delhi, 1967.

Ghosh, Sunit, *Orissa in Turmoil*, Cuttack, 1977.

Government of India, *The First Five Year Plan*, 1952.

——, *The Second Five Year Plan*, 1956.

——, *The Third Five Year Plan*, 1962.

——, *The Fourth Five Year Plan*, 1969.

Hanger, Welles, *After Nehru Who?*, London, 1963.

Humphrey, Berkeley, *Crossing the Floor*, Allen Unwin, 1972.

Jena, B.B., *Orissa, People and Government*.

Jennings, Sir Ivor, *Cabinet Government*, London, 1969.

Karunakaran, K.P., *Modern Indian Political Tradition*, Bombay, 1962.

Kashyap, S.C., *The Politics of Defections*, New Delhi, 1970.

Kashyap, S.C., *Anti Defection Laws and Parliamentary Privileges*, Bombay, 1993.

Khanna, H.R., *Report on the Commission of Inquiry*, 1967.

Mahtab, H.K., *History of Orissa*, Vol. II, Cuttack, 1960.

Mahtab, H.K., *The Beginning of the End*, Cuttack, 1971.

Mahtab, H.K., *Autobiography* (in Oriya).

Mahapatra, Jadunath, *Orissa in 1936-37 to 1938-39*, Cuttack, 1941.

Mahapatra, J.K., *Factional Politics in India*.

Mishra, Godavaris, *Autobiography* (in Oriya), Cuttack, 1952.

Mishra, P.K., *Political History of Orissa*, 1900-1936, New Delhi, 1979.

Mitter, G.K., *Report of the Commission of Inquiry*, 1974.

Mudholkar, J.R., *Inquiry Report*, 1970.

Myrdal, Gunnar, *Asian Drama*, 1968.

Nanda, S., *Coalitional Politics in Orissa*, New Delhi, 1979.

Narain, Iqbal (ed.), *State Politics in India*, Meerut.

Orissa Legislative Assembly, *Proceedings 1952-1999*.

Orissa Legislative Assembly, *Who is Who,* Bhubaneswar, 1996.

Padhi, K.S., *Corruption in Politics,* Delhi, 1986.

Patel, Sardar, *My Political Memories,* Nagpur, 1959.

Patnaik, B.K., *Politics of Floor Crossing.*

Pradhan, Pabitramohan, *Autobiography* (in Oriya), Cuttack, 1972.

Pye and Verba, *Political Culture and Political Development,* 1969.

Rajni Kothari, *Politics in India,* Orient Longman.

Rao, P.V.R., *Red Tape and White Cap,* New Delhi, 1970.

Rath, S.N., *The Development of the Welfare State in Orissa,* New Delhi, 1977.

RILT Service, *Decisions from the Chair (1937-94),* Bubaneswar, 1995.

Roy, Ramashray, *Uncertain Verdict: A Study of 1969 Elections in Four Indian States,* Longman, 1972.

Roy, Ramashray et al, *Relations Between Politician and Administrators,* New Delhi, 1969.

Sarjoo Prasad, *Report of the Commission of Inquiry,* 1972.

Sinha, K.K., *Ideology and Politics in India,* Calcutta, 1973.

Toub, Richard P., *Bureaucrats Under Stress,* Calcutta, 1969.

Tiwari, A.N., *Reference Orissa,* Bhubaneswar, 1999.

Index